SPECIAL
the story of the Unsinkable Daniel Cline

JOY CLINE

Copyright © 2025 Joy Cline.

All rights reserved. No part of this book may be used or reproduced by any means, graphic, electronic, or mechanical, including photocopying, recording, taping or by any information storage retrieval system without the written permission of the author except in the case of brief quotations embodied in critical articles and reviews.

This book is a work of non-fiction. Unless otherwise noted, the author and the publisher make no explicit guarantees as to the accuracy of the information contained in this book and in some cases, names of people and places have been altered to protect their privacy.

WestBow Press books may be ordered through booksellers or by contacting:

WestBow Press
A Division of Thomas Nelson & Zondervan
1663 Liberty Drive
Bloomington, IN 47403
www.westbowpress.com
844-714-3454

Because of the dynamic nature of the Internet, any web addresses or links contained in this book may have changed since publication and may no longer be valid. The views expressed in this work are solely those of the author and do not necessarily reflect the views of the publisher, and the publisher hereby disclaims any responsibility for them.

Any people depicted in stock imagery provided by Getty Images are models, and such images are being used for illustrative purposes only. Certain stock imagery © Getty Images.

Scripture quotations marked NIV are taken from The Holy Bible, New International Version®, NIV® Copyright © 1973, 1978, 1984, 2011 by Biblica, Inc.® Used by permission. All rights reserved worldwide.

ISBN: 979-8-3850-4357-6 (sc)
ISBN: 979-8-3850-4359-0 (hc)
ISBN: 979-8-3850-4358-3 (e)

Library of Congress Control Number: 2025901927

Print information available on the last page.

WestBow Press rev. date: 03/25/2025

CONTENTS

Acknowledgements ix

1	Shift	1
2	A Child Like No Other	7
3	Fitting In	15
4	A Shattered Future	19
5	No Room At The Inn	25
6	What's *Really* Important Anyway	36
7	Waymaker	43
8	A Family Affair	49
9	Vulnerabilities	57
10	A Different Kind of Education	67
11	Rising	73
12	Embedded Securities	93
13	The Third Option	104
14	Growing Pains	122
15	Good As Gold	140
16	Stretching	154
17	A Faith All His Own	169
18	Another Way To Worship	178
19	Thankful for Thin Walls	196
20	Having People	221
21	Flight	231

Epilogue 235
Disclaimer 237

TO DANIEL,

**without whom there is no story,
and to his indomitable spirit
that is truly unsinkable.**

**Love you!
Mom**

ACKNOWLEDGEMENTS

For my trio of encouragers: Geoff, Lyn, and Dawn, who never stopped asking—even though it dragged on—and who prodded me to the finish line, helping me believe I could do this hard thing,

For our friends and small groups over the years, who faithfully carried our burdens before the throne,

For Godmother Lois, who was there at Daniel's birth and has been there every step of the way since with her treasured prayers and letters,

For Allison, who came along at just the right time and made us all better by rescuing us from the ruts,

For MJ and all future MJs, who carry on the torch of Jesus to the next generation...cling to it and lift it high,

For Mary and Ben, who lived the story and who bear compassion's markings from it...I'm so very proud of you and honored by who you have become,

For Daniel, who continues to teach me by example to put people first...

love you all!

And to God, who made this all possible...
to You be the glory!

"Great is the Lord and most worthy of praise;
his greatness no one can fathom.
One generation commends your works to another;
they tell of your mighty acts.
They speak of the glorious splendor of your majesty—
and I will meditate on your wonderful works.
They tell of the power of your awesome works—
and I will proclaim your great deeds.
They celebrate your abundant goodness
and joyfully sing of your righteousness."

Psalm 145:3-7 NIV

1

SHIFT

One of my favorite books is Dick Foth's *Known,* a book based on the premise that one of our deepest needs as humans is relationships where we intentionally seek to know others and be vulnerable enough that we might be known by them.[1] It's a premise that has served me well across the years as I have cultivated those core friendships in my life who are all-access friends into my soul, and I into theirs.

And so it was as Geoff and I jettisoned off into wedded bliss in the fall of 1990 that we established a foundational value of surrounding ourselves with committed relationships—a small group—with whom we would do life. It was a decision from which we have rarely strayed across our thirty-four years of marriage.

In those early days, Tuesdays were the evenings we would part ways—Geoff to his group of guys and I to my ladies. They were groups that looked much like us—young, recently married individuals who loved Jesus and were trying to figure how to honor Him through this new life as couples. We shared struggles, we shared victories, we shared Scripture, and we shared recipes. We laughed together, cried together, and challenged, encouraged, and prayed for one another.

Amidst all this sharing, it wasn't long before we shared another facet of life together—pregnancy. Angela became pregnant

---

[1] Foth, D. (2017). *Known: Finding deep friendships in a shallow world.* WaterBrook.

first, and then it was Karen. Soon our small group wasn't so small any longer as infants Christine and Christopher joined our Tuesday evenings, and we were now sharing arms with which to cradle them. Far greater from these evenings was shared a seed of desire that Geoff's and my family might be enlarged as well, a desire that only intensified as soon thereafter both Lori and Karin became pregnant as well. Our Tuesdays became abuzz of all things babies with a little Jesus sprinkled in, and I was suddenly feeling very much on the outside. As weeks turned into months of anticipation, only to be followed closely by disappointment, I began wondering if something might be wrong with me. I'm thankful in those days that I didn't have WebMD to fuel those fears. My disappointment that seemed so monumental at the time was relatively short-lived though, as spring brought the sprouting of that embedded seed of desire: Geoff and I found we were expecting in the fall. And with that, suddenly Tuesdays became meaningful again as I had so much to learn.

What I didn't pick up from those Tuesday small groups, I found in the pages of a trending book, *What to Expect When You're Expecting* by Heidi Murkoff.[2] I was captivated by the book's answers to questions I either never thought to ask, or was too embarrassed to ask in my naïveté. My mom had passed away before I had even met Geoff, and as I awaited the birth of what would have been her first grandchild, I missed her all the more keenly. She would have loved to have been a grandma and would have embraced her new role with her patented zeal for life. The book did help fill in the gaps, and I was fascinated, in particular, with the stages of development of my baby and my own pregnant self. But somewhere in the pages of the book, my sense of anticipation gave way to fear. Maybe it

---

[2] Murkoff, H., Mazel, S., & Neppe, C. (2018). *What to expect when you're expecting.* HarperCollins Publishers.

SPECIAL

was the detailing of all that could go wrong in pregnancy and in the baby's development, maybe it was all those prenatal appointments and my own diagnosis of asthma during the early days of my pregnancy, or maybe it was watching a friend's coming-to-terms with her fourth child's future and trajectory that looked much different from the daughter's siblings for the disabilities that were becoming apparent. Whatever the case, my happy-go-lucky, couldn't-wait-to-be-a-mom days suddenly were clouded by an impending sense of worry over the "*what if's*": what if my baby has physical limitations, what if my baby is slowed developmentally, what if my baby bears markings that isolate him or her, what if my baby dies. The "*what if's*" seemed endless, and they chased my mind into dark corners of anxiety.

And so it was under these auspices I set off for home after a day of teaching. Just blocks from school, I was abruptly stopped by a school bus's flashing stop sign. As the bus door swung open, a rather large group of elementary students piled off the bus breaking into smaller groupings of two to three... heads down, content in the company of peers. The parents, who had been chatting away with one another, quickly fell in line behind their children in a mass exodus homeward. But one boy in particular caught my eye for how he stood in contrast to the rest of the group: he was alone, his eyes locked on his mom who stood at a distance waiting. He took off racing towards her in a loping gait, wrapping his arms around her in a fierce embrace. She was his world. He began pulling things from his backpack—artwork and papers, the prizes of his day—to show his mom and to absorb her affirmation. Soon they were the only two left, as the other students, parents, and even the bus had moved on. As I began to move on as well, I took one last look and recognized the unmistakable characteristics of Down syndrome in the boy's features.

JOY CLINE

In the days that followed my bus encounter, the scene replayed over and over in my mind, leaving me wrestling with God. What *if* my baby had Down syndrome or was disabled in some fashion, this very thing I feared? That bus scene seemed to call out my anxieties with answers I had never considered: I would have a child less harbored by peer dependency, a child who loved and depended on me, a child unencumbered by the trappings of all this world offers, a child devoted to me. Who wouldn't want that kind of relationship with their child? The truth of that special relationship chased down my *"what-ifs,"* rendering them powerless in their attacks. And in that wrestling, God worked in my mind and heart a paradoxical shift over that which had stirred fear to that which I accepted... even welcomed.

With fear's grip broken, I powered through those final months of pregnancy with unabashed anticipation, able to finish *What to Expect When You're Expecting* with expectations of joy at this new life God had for us that would indeed make us a family. The bus scene seared in my memory, I readied myself in prayer for what seemed to me the inevitable—so real and so raw in its lesson.

Yet when—on October 8, 1992—we welcomed Mary into our world, I was overjoyed—yet puzzled—that she was so absolutely perfect in every way imaginable. We were in love. But in the back of my mind, so vivid was the experience that aligned my heart and will with the Lord's, I questioned the whole validity of the bus scene: What was that about, Lord? I was ready. To be sure, we were to find out that Mary's supposed perfection came with a heart defect that led us to a pediatric heart specialist within weeks of her birth. But

4

even in the anxieties we held for the fragility of our newborn daughter, I had a certainty this was not the fulfillment of the bus scene surrender. This was different.

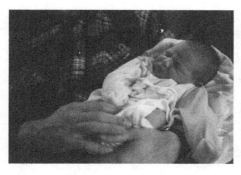

On April 7, 1994, nearly eighteen months to the day after Mary's birth, Ben was born. And our family of three became one of four—much to the distress of Mary, who rattled the hospital's hallway with her despairing laments at first sight of her baby brother in my arms. She was definitely not a fan, but he grew on her. Heck! He grew on all of us! Ben was easygoing, smiley, content, and whole. He, as well, defied my bus scene prediction for our family. My heart, which was once again steeled for my *"what if,"* was thankful for the birth of another healthy child.

"Are you ready to be a dad again?" With those words, shock registered on Geoff's face. Mary was just over two years old, and Ben was ten months old at the time. We were about to be outnumbered.

On September 19, 1995, Daniel made a dramatic entrance, as the umbilical cord became wrapped around his neck at birth. As Geoff was pushed back, doctors flew into action and were quickly able to restore his breathing as his piercing cries reached my ears with their reassurance. It wasn't long before they placed him in my arms: ten fingers, ten toes, a beautiful placid face, and another perfect son.

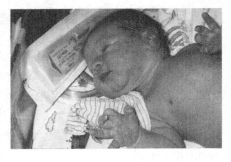

The Cline family now boasted five strong, and we knew it was complete, despite our pre-marriage musings of five children. Three children under the age of three have a way of altering your best-laid plans. As we settled into life as that complete family of five, I began to doubt the significance of the school bus scene with its lesson of yielding to God's higher plans. What meaning did it hold for me any longer? After all, I had my perfect family.

2
A CHILD LIKE NO OTHER

All of our children have solid biblical names: Mary, Benjamin, and Daniel. In naming them, we wanted to somehow impart the legacy of the person behind the name. Thus, Mary was named for Mary, the mother of Jesus—a nod to our early days in the Catholic Church. But even more so, Geoff and I marveled at the biblical Mary's humble yielding to God's higher plans for her, despite the humiliating high personal cost. We wanted that same humble yielding to mark our firstborn daughter. To be sure, our Mary often lamented being saddled with such an "old-fashioned" name—at least she didn't have to battle name recognition as the only Mary in her graduating class!

For Ben, we had an entirely different approach in naming him, choosing the *meaning* of the name to dictate our selection, more so than the person. Benjamin means "son of his father's right hand." In naming the son of his old age, Jacob probably desired that special connection with his youngest son. That was our heart as well. We wanted Ben to literally be Geoff's right-hand little man.

7

JOY CLINE

When I was in college, I had a plant known as a "prayer plant" in my dorm room. With its characteristic leaves that faithfully opened and closed at the day's beginning and end, it served for me a visual reminder to take time to pray during those very full days. I named the plant Daniel. Ten years later, it still seemed the perfect name—not just for a plant, but for our newborn son. The Daniel exiled to Babylon was one who stood out in a hostile setting: from the confidence to advocate for himself, to the convictions that grounded him, to his ability to rise above peer dependency, to his prayer life that was both faithful and faith-filled. Those were the exact characteristics we wanted to mark our Daniel, and so the name stuck. To be sure, over the years Daniel would collect many nicknames, the result of having a dad who rarely stuck to his students' given names—Daniel Do, Weeeeeeeee Buddy, and the Unsinkable Daniel Cline. I especially liked the latter, a nod to his sunny personality that rallied even in the grimmest of days.

SPECIAL

As that third child under three years old, Daniel entered a world that was a beehive of activity. Some would call it chaotic. I experienced the grounding of my mobility with Mary, such was the seeming enormity of getting an infant out the door in my early days of motherhood. By the time I had Daniel, I was a seasoned mom adept at getting three young ones, all with very different agendas, aligned and moving in the same direction.

Daniel was our child who was dragged everywhere. It was to be his lot in life as the baby of the family to be carted along to church activities, homeschool co-op, music lessons, sporting events, and countless recitals and concerts—most of which were not his own. But he bore it well with a compliant, adaptive personality that was content to be in the center of all the action. Perhaps this is the reason Daniel remains the only pure extrovert in the Cline family.

Daniel's early days began so seemingly normal. There was nothing to mark him as anything less than that "perfect" son we brought into the world on September 19, 1995. It would be months before those first fissures in the facade began to emerge, giving me pause at this child's differentness.

It began with food, which is such an amazing thought for what an important role food now plays in Daniel's life. When I began to transition him to solid foods from nursing, he wanted nothing of it! Feeding time, normally a pleasurable experience for most babies, became a battlefield for us. Daniel turned his nose at most foods. It was a texture thing. And so my days became a search for anything he might tolerate. We finally settled on four foods: Gerber baby food jars of bananas, carrots, squash, and sweet potatoes. That was it! As Daniel grew older, I tried to mash the actual bananas, carrots, squash, and sweet potatoes; but they were never smooth enough for his tongue's liking. I was always trying to sneak into these jars of baby food nutrients that might add substance and protein. Eventually peanut butter became something he not only tolerated, but loved, and still does to this day. Still, it wasn't much of a diet, and this went on until he was a toddler. In fact, I remember trying to feed him crumbled chocolate cake for his second birthday and reducing him to screaming tears.

All this lack of nutrition had its effect. There was a listlessness to him, and he was the slowest of our kids to begin walking at just over fourteen months. He also resorted heavily to exploring his world through licking. He would lick balls, toys, bats...the things most children would play with. And yet while all these stood out as different from our other children, they weren't beyond explainable...or so I tried to convince myself.

SPECIAL

At his eighteen-month checkup, none of these raised a red flag of enormous alarm for Daniel's pediatrician, Dr. Daniel Dufort, a wonderful doctor who made going to the doctor an enjoyable experience with his kindness, humor, and talking parrot. What did alarm Dr. Dufort were two things: Daniel's eyesight and his sparse speaking. He recommended two appointments—an eye appointment and an evaluation by the Fraser Institute of Minneapolis.

And so it was that Dr. Evan Ballard, a pediatric ophthalmologist, entered Daniel's life with his corny jokes and antics with a mechanical dog that kept Daniel entertained just long enough to enable him to complete an eye exam. The diagnosis, in layman's terms, was farsightedness. I still recall the day we picked up Daniel's new glasses at the mall. The glasses had such thick lenses that they resembled the bottoms of old-fashioned pop bottles. Wise parents that we were, we added an adjustable strap to these glasses before leaving the store to keep them from falling off his face or from him pulling them off. Little were we to worry about the latter, for as we emerged from the LensCrafters, I watched my nineteen-month old son wheel around in my arms, eyes wide in wonderment. I had no doubt that these new glasses had literally opened his eyes to a new world. They also earned him a new moniker, Little Ralphie, after the eldest son in the Christmas classic *A Christmas Story*. With his sandy blonde hair and prominent glasses, Daniel struck a stunning resemblance to Ralphie.

The second appointment wasn't quite as settling. I had my radar up for this one, as I found the Fraser Institute was a healthcare system catering to individuals with autism and other disabilities. What I remember most from that appointment was the play-time evaluation Geoff and I were privy to behind a two-sided mirror. As I watched the evaluator's attempts to engage Daniel, I did so with a mindset in denial, seeking

JOY CLINE

flaws with which to dismiss its inevitable conclusions. It was no surprise when we received the results of the session that labeled Daniel as on the autism spectrum. At the time, autism was a relatively rare diagnosis, though it had been prevalent for years under alternate labeling attempts and was on the cusp of exploding. As such, understanding was sparse and only just emerging. One bit of early information that I held doggedly to as a defense against Daniel's diagnosis were articles noting the lack of a cure for autism and the inability to grow and improve from its clutches. I saw growth and change in Daniel, and dismissed his diagnosis based on this misleading understanding.

Even while in denial, I did agree to therapies for Daniel. I knew we needed help. Soon our weeks filled up with sensory and speech appointments. Most of the sensory therapies seemed laughable at the time, as they sought to desensitize him to different stimuli. One had us placing a near naked Daniel into a very large tub of rice to play. Many had him exploring a variety of texture-rich toys. His speech deficiencies, we found, were attributed to his slow transition to solid foods that required him to chew and engage tongue and mouth muscles in new ways. As such, his speech therapies were coordinated with feeding strategies that both sought to advance him.

In time, steady progress was made which only solidified our hope that Daniel would "catch up" and defy his label. However, the autism label continued to chase us down as the Farmington School District came knocking to test Daniel for their Early Childhood Special Education program. As an ardent homeschool mom, I wanted nothing to do with the local school district. But as a rule-follower, I couldn't find a way to deny access to our son. And so it was on a summer day in 1998, two representatives from the school district were at our front door to evaluate Daniel for their program.

SPECIAL

Much like the Fraser evaluation from a year earlier, the school district did much of its testing through the use of toys, manipulatives, and pictures, as I sat watching from a nearby couch. If I found fault with the Fraser evaluation, I questioned the practices, procedures, and eventual results of the school district's assessment even more so. Daniel, ever the people pleaser, seemed to have a disconnect with these women. He was distracted and distressed at being pulled from his typical morning routines, and they were unable to engage him in meaningful play. It was a disaster. The results from the assessment bore that disconnect, and the district added another label to Daniel—developmentally delayed—and recommended that he begin their Early Childhood Special Education program in the fall.

For some time I raged against the techniques of the evaluators, before time and Geoff's words had their softening effect, enabling me in the very least to entertain the thought of sending Daniel off to early school. Admittedly, the thought was tempting, as I knew it would afford me focused time with Mary and Ben in those all-important first years of homeschooling. Coinciding with this thought was our meeting of Daniel's potential teacher, Miss Jen. Miss Jen was everything the district evaluators were not: compassionate, kind, nurturing, engaging, gentle, and quick to laugh. She took a genuine interest in Daniel, and I saw him respond to her. Daniel has always been an amazing judge of character. I relented.

And so it was that morning of September 8, 1998, Daniel and I awaited the little bus that would take him off to school—the first Cline child to do so. As is true of all first mornings, the bus seemed long in arriving. No doubt I spent those extra moments overwhelming Daniel with first-day reminders, even as I tried to reassure him—never a great mix. I think I was just as much trying to reassure myself that Geoff and I were

JOY CLINE

doing the right thing by putting him on that bus. It just seemed so wrong, homeschool mom that I was, to be entrusting my youngest and most vulnerable into the clutches of an outside world where I had no oversight or control. I fought mightily the emotions of that morning, trying to remain strong and in control for Daniel's sake. He didn't need to see my struggle.

At long last the moment arrived. The bus stopped at our driveway and swung open its door. We exchanged introductions with the bus driver and aide, and Daniel climbed the steps of the bus, his large, red backpack fairly toppling over his small stature. He seemed way too young for all of this at two years, eleven months.

As the bus pulled away and I watched my little boys' big, trusting eyes speed away, I was dissolved to tears. There's something monumental in that moment of exchange for a mom—the untethering of a bond long bound in time. It's no wonder it's become one of the most photographed moments of childhood. I had no camera. It was not a moment I wished to capture for posterity. In fact, I spent much of the rest of that morning wishing I could erase it from my memory and praying the Lord would care for him from afar as we entrusted Daniel into His higher care.

3

FITTING IN

If I had moments of doubt whether Geoff and I were doing the right thing by putting Daniel on the bus that first morning of school, I was in full-blown retreat mode as the hours stretched awaiting his return. In the span of that seeming eternity, I had all sorts of imaginings and fears. They kept me churning. They kept me praying. I expected—or maybe I secretly hoped—Daniel would be a wreck when he got off that bus that first day of school, proof this whole school thing was a sham and providing fodder for me to bring him back to the safety and security of home.

But a funny thing happened: Daniel emerged from the bus that day with a big smile on his face, no worse for the wear from school's torturing. While he lacked the ability to detail the events of his day, his smile and exuberance spoke volumes that school had not dampened my boy's zest and zeal for life. After all, he was the Unsinkable Daniel Cline!

In his backpack that day, I found a notebook that was to become our lifeline for that year of school, bridging the gap of Daniel's lack of communication and thrilling us with insights into his days at school. Ms. Jen was faithful to make Daniel's days come alive with her recounting, and they became the safety ring to which I clung. Most days I marveled at skills he was acquiring, while other days I wept for the struggle of it all.

JOY CLINE

You would think Daniel's emergence from the bus that day would have conjured a sense of fulfillment from that bus scene I had come upon six years earlier, so profound the impact it had on me. Amazingly, it did not. At this point, I still did not connect Daniel to that little boy with Down syndrome. I didn't even see Daniel as disabled in any way. After all, in his labeling—developmentally delayed—did that not portend it was merely a matter of time before he would catch up?

Bus rides would become one of Daniel's favorite parts of school, so much so that his favorite toys from this age were Fisher Price and Little Tykes school buses that he would push around the house, picking up and dropping off passengers— one that bore a strong resemblance to him. Perhaps it was the routine and predictability of the bus route that Daniel found so grounding in his autistic nature, or maybe it was the consistent interactions with the bus driver, aide, parents, and fellow students that fed him. Whatever the case, Daniel loved his bus rides!

Daniel is our extrovert. He is always looking for ways to interact with others. He just always didn't know how to make that happen. In the early years, when communication was particularly challenging for Daniel, we taught him some basic sign language to enable him to express his needs—none more important than "more" for a boy for whom food was becoming increasingly important.

As Daniel continued his school journey, we found it difficult to give him the tools he needed to have those meaningful interactions with others that he so craved. It often came in the form of coaching him to ask a starter question. One of his favorite go-to questions was: What did you have for breakfast? He asked this every day of every person, and each new day brought another opportunity to ask it all over again. Despite coaching, Daniel rarely got beyond the topic of food, and was unable to carry the conversation beyond its inception.

At school they worked to help Daniel assimilate with his peers by introducing him to social stories. Social stories are a teaching strategy that employs images and role playing. They

JOY CLINE

gave Daniel the tools to better navigate social interactions and to help him read faces to better understand the emotional context of his conversations.

It was about this time that an unwanted behavior began to crop up that would follow Daniel to this day—copying. He would especially copy the insignificant, often overlooked actions of others. When someone coughed, Daniel coughed. When someone burped, Daniel burped. When someone took off their glasses, he did the same. He would even copy someone who tripped and fell down. I believe in Daniel's mind that copying brought the attention and interaction he craved, however negative. Copying was a way he integrated himself into the lives of others, making himself like them, even while annoying them.

Eventually, this pursuit of interaction through copying took a more serious turn, exposing Daniel's vulnerability at the hands of those with whom he sought friendship. People pleaser that he is, Daniel was willing to do almost anything to win the acceptance of others. Third grade Daniel followed the conjolings of his playground peers in surprising a girl with a kiss on a dare, middle school Daniel gave away his prized Nintendo DS and joined another in trashing a sibling's bedroom, and college Daniel willingly took his roommate's picture in the nude at his request and texted it to a housing mentor—all in the name of "friendship" and all coming at a high cost in consequences. Daniel was learning, often the hard way.

4

A SHATTERED FUTURE

Even as I continued to homeschool Mary and Ben, Daniel continued to board the bus for an education that was uniquely his. His school days were a mixture of a traditional school setting in the mornings with his afternoons at home—a mixture we felt was perfect for Daniel. It offered him the extra help he needed at school through special services like speech and occupational therapy. It built in a more intensive, small group skill-building time. Maybe most importantly, it provided him the interactions he so craved with his traditional classmates during morning circle time and enrichment classes like music, art, and gym. Afternoons at home, I was able to spend one-on-one time with him on the basics.

If Daniel's days had a transient nature to them, his educational journey was even more uprooting. While living in the same house throughout all his school years, Daniel shifted schools six times during his tenure in the Farmington Public Schools! Though hardly ideal, especially for a young boy with autism, I think Daniel gained an adaptability that defied his autistic tendencies. He learned to navigate new places and found joy in new faces. And with each changing landscape conquered, his confidence and circle grew a little larger.

Despite the ever-altering educational landscape for Daniel, one element became a fixture of his educational journey: the annual IEP meeting. An IEP, or Individualized Education Program, details the services and adaptations a disabled

JOY CLINE

student receives. It charts objectives for the student's growth in assorted areas, the measurements used to assess progress, and the results gathered from observations and testing. Geoff and I were annually treated to this rite of passage for all parents of special education children. And with each passing meeting and each passing year, hope for Daniel's future was slowly being extinguished by an ever-emerging glass ceiling.

To be fair, I honestly don't remember a whole lot from those early IEP meetings. A stack of paperwork greeted us at each of them, along with all the teachers and support staff that filled Daniel's days at school. On cue, each of them took turns rattling off their portion of the stack: Daniel will correctly articulate his beginning "I" sound in 8 of 10 attempts as observed through three separate trials; Daniel will hop on one foot five feet across the floor on three separate attempts as observed; Daniel will not laugh at or copy a peer's actions as observed in a classroom setting across three separate trials. The bar seemed so low, and Geoff and I flitted between disbelief—Can he *really* not do that?—to dogged determination—He *will* do that!—to desperation—Will he *ever* do that?

As we pondered these questions and fought to defy them, one IEP meeting stood in contrast—not only for its "answers," but also for whom was in attendance.

Daniel was in third grade at Meadowview Elementary and settling in nicely as he hit a stretch of more than a year in the same educational setting. Geoff and I had a skip to our step as we entered the school that day. We really believed in the autism program Daniel was enrolled in and were even more impressed with the teachers that coaxed Daniel's best out of him. As we entered the room, we saw those faces we had come to know and depend on for Daniel's school days, but we also saw an unfamiliar one. And while the face was unknown,

SPECIAL

the name was not. In attendance that day was a name that graced the stacks of all of Daniel's IEP paperwork: Beth Langston, director of special education for the Farmington school district. And with that introduction, the meeting took on an added insistence and authority.

Beth was not a woman of stature. In fact, she was not that much taller than nine-year-old Daniel. But what she lacked in stature, she more than made up with an aura of preeminence. So while the others fell in line parading through their portion of the stack, it was Beth's voice at the end that spoke the loudest and had the most lasting impact on me: "Daniel will be lucky if he can read common traffic signs, like a stop sign, when he is older." I was dumbfounded. I was devastated. I was defiant. All that work with him…was it really not making a dent? Was I kidding myself trying to teach him? I was so sure he was *already* reading more than road signs, but I wasn't the expert. I wasn't the authority in the room. It was the first time I really had to concede that "developmentally delayed" didn't necessarily translate into Daniel "catching up," as I had always believed he would. More than anything we had heard thus far in Daniel's educational journey, those words spoke of a death over the dreams Geoff and I had for our boy.

Dazed and disheartened, we spent the rest of the meeting nodding our heads in resignation as Beth proceeded to cast a vision for us to consider placing Daniel in a group home to spend his adult years. A group home. And all this at nine years old. It was too much to take in. We left the meeting deflated by a future that had been painted for us that was vastly different from the future we had envisioned even as recently as when we had entered the school that day. The skip was definitely gone.

Geoff is a middle school teacher. He loves teaching middle schoolers, dorky as they are, and they love him. I had spent

JOY CLINE

much of my teaching career as a middle school teacher, as well, prior to becoming a stay-at-home mom. There's nothing like teaching in the middle schools to reinforce that middle school is not for the faint of heart. So it wasn't surprising that Geoff and I made the decision, even before we were married, that we wanted to homeschool our kids. We wanted to speak truth over who they were in Christ and allow God to define their sense of self-worth, not their peers, particularly through the critical middle school years.

As Mary and Ben began successfully navigating their middle school years—still homeschooled, but attending music and Spanish classes in the schools—we heard their cries for greater autonomy and independence. We revisited our premarital plans and sheepishly acquiesced to allowing them to choose whether or not they entered the public schools as eighth graders. While we felt they were as ready as they could be, we let out an audible sigh of relief when, apart from one other, they each decided to continue homeschooling that year. We weren't quite as fortunate the next year. When afforded the chance to go into the schools full time as ninth graders, they both jumped at it. And we gulped, for ninth grade in the Farmington Schools at that time was still part of the middle school.

Meanwhile Daniel, ever on his own educational journey, was nearing the start of his middle school years. The teachers, who we had learned to trust over the years, were now eyeing Daniel's transition into middle school. At the time, Daniel was still spending part of his day at Meadowview and part of it at home. They reasoned with us that Daniel, as an autistic child, needed that exposure to the varied and comprehensive social interactions he would have as a full time student in middle school in order to grow. Middle school would afford Daniel the multiple social interactions that home did not. Middle school...

SPECIAL

the very place we strategized to shield our children from, yet here we were considering sending Daniel, our most vulnerable, into its throws. Middle school is hard. Add a disability in there, and it is harder still. We prayed over this decision...earnestly. We stewed over it just as earnestly. Ultimately, we yielded. Daniel was going to Farmington Middle School East, a building housing only sixth and seventh graders.

While I'd like to say that this transition to full time schooling in middle school was a smooth one, there were days when we questioned our sanity in sending him. To be sure, Daniel was mostly loving his days, ripe with all the social interactions he could pack in them. The interplay of those interactions was where it sometimes got messy. And I was about to find out just how messy, as we had another IEP meeting circled prominently on the family calendar.

This time, however, I entered the school building solo and with a fair bit of trepidation, as Geoff had a commitment that afternoon he couldn't break. We always attended these meetings together and presented that united front. Through our more than thirty years of marriage I have come to understand how I am strengthened and buoyed simply by Geoff's presence in such situations. I deeply missed him that day. A roomful of eyes shifted to me as I entered the meeting, and I very much felt the weight of going it alone.

Geoff has always held to the motto that for every hard word you must convey, always preempt it with two positive ones. This motto has served him well as a middle school teacher. It must be a middle school teacher thing, this motto thing, for it seemed the teachers in the room that day embraced the same motto. They gave me some Daniel Cline moments that made me smile and beam in the retelling, but always following closely on the heels were moments that made me cringe

JOY CLINE

and sink. The evaluations, the testing, the observations, and the stories compounded upon one another. A picture was painted of classmates' interactions and responses to Daniel that broke my heart for the reality of the daily battles that were his that I didn't even know about. While I don't remember the specifics of what was said in that IEP meeting, I do remember my response as I was made privy to Daniel's days. I wept. I wept for my son's struggles and challenges, so exposed in the recounting of his teachers. Daniel's struggles were every bit my own, and I felt every bit a failure as a mom for being unable to shield him. The problems were increasing and intensifying, unearthed by a middle school environment that was far from kind. As the tears flowed, I tried mightily to hide them and compose myself to utter a few intelligible words.

That was the last IEP meeting I ever attended on my own. It was also the first time I allowed myself to believe that Daniel was, perhaps, the fulfillment of the bus scene of so many years ago now.

5

NO ROOM AT THE INN

One of the best decisions we made in our kids' educational journey was to join a homeschool co-op. Ours was Southern Cross Christian Co-op, and it met a couple of Tuesday afternoons each month for enrichment classes and support. A co-op can take on many shapes and sizes. Southern Cross was Christian-based and enrolled preschoolers to sixth graders, limiting the class sizes to around ten students per grade. It also gave parents the time to put their feet up and learn from one another on assorted topics. That equated to about forty families converging on South Suburban E-Free Church every other Tuesday. While the classes offered help to round out the limitations of schooling at home—particularly in the case of a gym class—the greatest benefits of the co-op for our family were the relationships and connections we would make on what most outsiders view as an "isolated" journey.

Our co-op journey began in the fall of 1999, as I herded second grader Mary, first grader Ben, and preschooler Daniel into the church where the co-op rented space, depositing each of them at their designated classroom. Mary and Ben had it relatively easy. They were in the same classroom together, as first and second graders rotated together to each of their classes. Daniel was on his own without a familiar face in sight as I left him in the care of Ms. Beth. Ms. Beth was not only the preschool teacher, but also a co-op parent. She had the help of a teenage assistant, the sibling of one of our co-op's homeschool families. With ten three and four-year olds, she

JOY CLINE

would need all the help she could get! If ever having Daniel in her class was too much for her, Ms. Beth never let on.

We quickly embraced and anticipated our every-other-Tuesday-afternoon routine. So much so, that when the time came to re-enroll for the next year, we were all in. The drop-off that year added another stop. Mary, as a third grader, was now part of the third and fourth grade rotation, while Ben remained with the first/second grade bunch and Daniel bumped up to Kindergarten 4/5. Homeschoolers fiercely embrace their independence in educating their children as they see fit. The K 4/5 class was a by-product of that independence, offering parents the flexibility of holding their child back for another year of preschool or moving them on to kindergarten. While I'm sure being in denial somewhat played a part in our decision to have four-year-old Daniel graduate to the kindergarten classroom, I'm sure there also might have been a numbers game going on as well. The co-op was pretty firm about capping the class size of the younger classes.

Whatever the reason, Daniel found himself in Mrs. Doffing's kindergarten. Mrs. Doffing was a saint. Although she wasn't an SCCC mom, she *was* a homeschool mom. She brought a couple of her daughters along each week to help with the class. Daniel loved Mrs. Doffing. She was nurturing, she was grace-filled, and she was seasoned. As such, she loved Daniel, and loved him through his inabilities. She took a special interest in him and worked hard so that his deficiencies weren't so stark against the rest of the class. It was a sad last day when we learned—after two years in Mrs. Doffing's Kindergarten 4/5–that she was not returning to teach in the fall. As special needs parents, we seem to regularly brush up against such saints who come alongside us for a season to get us to the other side of our seeming mountains, better for their handprint upon it. Mrs. Doffing was one of those.

SPECIAL

But now Daniel was six, and it was inevitable he joined the first/second grade rotation of classes with the rest of his peers...or was it? Remember what I said about homeschoolers being a fiercely independent bunch? By now it was clear Daniel was not ready for the rigors of rotating to three academic classes. Coincidentally, I had risen in the co-op ranks to now serve as co-administrator. As such, one of my roles was to hire teachers, and we had an opening in kindergarten. I turned to a good friend of mine who, incidentally, was Daniel's first teacher at church. Maybe it was for selfish reasons that I hired Terri, but I like to think I'm a pretty good judge of character and heart. Terri had both, and I knew that as such, she would slip into the void of Mrs. Doffing with ease.

Somewhere in the hiring of Terri, I raised the question, exacting my homeschool independence best: Why *can't* Daniel stay in kindergarten another year? That's who God made him to be and where the learning was catered to him. Homeschool minds agreed. And so, Daniel became the first—and probably the only—three-time kindergartner in SCCC history, and I let out a sigh of relief knowing Daniel would be safe and loved under Terri's familiar guard.

27

JOY CLINE

However, after three years in kindergarten, it was time to face the music. Daniel was seven now—three weeks shy of turning eight—and entering second grade at school. No matter how "independent" homeschoolers are, an eight-year-old kindergartner wasn't going to fly. The gap had widened, and Daniel no longer fit in with his peers. As a family, we were torn. Mary and Ben were still widely benefiting from their co-op Tuesdays, particularly in regards to friend groups. As for me, I still had two years to go on my commitment as co-administrator for the co-op. Only Daniel didn't have a place any longer at SCCC.

And so began a new drop-off routine, one that had us swinging by Geoff's middle school en route to the co-op to drop Daniel off to spend his afternoon in the back of Geoff's seventh grade U.S. History class. I'm pretty sure having Daniel hanging out at school wasn't protocol, but we made it work with coloring books, books, games, and curious middle schoolers to entertain him and occupy his time. Isn't it ironic that while Daniel was able to spend his afternoons in a public middle school classroom, he was unable to fit into a Christian homeschool co-op classroom?

That was the canundrum I wrestled mightily with as I served out my final two years with the co-op. They were difficult years. My best friend and fellow co-administrator from my first year in the role had moved on from the co-op to substitute teaching. I also had trouble coming to terms with the high cost this position exacted from our family, both in the sheer time I spent in leading it and in the divisive nature of not having a place for my youngest son. A seed of resentment had been planted that I was never able to fully reconcile before we ended our days at SCCC.

Meanwhile, we were encountering some of the same hurdles at our church home, Woodcrest Church. We had found

SPECIAL

Woodcrest our first year at SCCC, probably due to the influence of several SCCC families who also called it their church home. We jumped into Woodcrest—not just with our right hand, left hand, right foot, left foot, or head, and shaking it all about—but with our whole bodies and souls. Geoff joined the youth ministry, and I found my niche in the children's ministry, co-teaching a third grade class on Sunday mornings. It was a rare season of teaching for me, as there was not a single Cline child in sight in my Sunday school classroom that first year at Woodcrest. I merely stepped in where the need was greatest, and that was third grade teaching alongside Ms. Ali, with whom I would forge a partnership in children's ministry for years. Mary and Ben would come along to my third grade class in subsequent years, but this year was uniquely Cline-less.

In the meantime, Daniel began in the preschool class at Woodcrest. I will never forget the first day we dropped him off–for into whose awaiting care would we entrust him, but Ms. Terri's. It was a first for us to leave Daniel in a Sunday school class. We usually brought him along to church with us at our old church. It was easier that way. Terri made the exchange just as easy. She got down on his level and welcomed Daniel with an enthusiasm and warmth that was genuine. There was a natural connection. We saw it and felt it that day, and we grew it into a deep friendship as families that has lasted to this day. As a homeschool family, we tried to cultivate every friendship-building experience we could get. That's why co-op and church were so important to us. Most of these relationships were the ones with whom our kids had play dates, and with whom they celebrated birthdays and the big events of life.

Daniel's journey through Sunday school began to resemble his co-op one. He went on to kindergarten at Woodcrest with little fanfare. But when it became time to move on to first grade

JOY CLINE

with his classmates, we balked. Besides Daniel's difficulty in keeping up with his peers as expectations increased, we also saw relational value in holding him back a year. Terri's son, Grant, who was a year behind Daniel in school, was going into kindergarten. Additionally, we had some twins from our family's small group that were entering kindergarten that year, along with a co-op boy with whom we were beginning to do things. It seemed a good fit. And so, Daniel began year two as a kindergartner at church.

As I reflect back on those days, it hurts me that of *all* places—the church and a Christian homeschool co-op—we experienced the greatest difficulty integrating Daniel. While this would change through the years, there were at the time few ministries reaching out to special needs children, embracing them and their parents into the hub of activity reserved for the traditional child. More often than not, parents of special needs children either didn't even attempt church, or did so in a limited fashion. Simply stated: there was no room at the inn. Somehow I think Jesus, who had his own first-hand experience with being the outcast, weeps over such exclusions.

By the time Daniel was due to graduate to first grade at church, Ben had moved on to fourth grade. Unstrapped from the family commitment to Mary and Ben, I made the leap from teaching third grade Sunday school to first, just so I could intentionally span the gap for Daniel by my mere presence in his classroom. This seemed to be working pretty well, or so I thought. One phone call would bring my perceived sense of altruism crashing down.

It was late afternoon on a Friday, and I was working on dinner and readying the family to get out the door for our biweekly family small group. We had been with the same small group now for over three years and were forging unbreakable bonds.

SPECIAL

Our nights together always began around the table over a meal or dessert, before splitting ways so the parents could study God's Word together while the kids played games and hung out. Besides a family of twins, there was also a family of quadruplets joining us and six other families. Some might call it chaotic with twelve adults and sixteen kids under roof, but I like to reflect back on those nights as sweet fellowship.These relationships became our core people for seven of the most foundational years of our family's lives.

When the phone rang that Friday afternoon, I was surprised to find Carol, a mom from both the co-op and church, on the other end of the line. Her daughter Elise had been in Daniel's class his last year at co-op and now was in his first grade Sunday school class. We exchanged pleasantries, but Carol wasn't one to beat around the bush. Nor was she one to mince words or exude Minnesota nice. Her words that day were pointed and directed at me in their venom. As one who also helped out at times in Daniel's and Elise's Sunday school class, she painted a picture that stripped the facade I conjured in my own mind that Daniel was holding his own amongst his younger classmates. She labeled us as selfish for having Daniel in the Sunday school classes, saying he took too much time and resources from the other children. She said that as such, he was limiting the experience and potential of the others in the class. She went on to name other mothers in the class who were in agreement with her. Further, she reflected back to the past year of co-op, describing Daniel's presence in his final year of kindergarten as detrimental to the students there as well. Her words attacked me on so many levels: as a mom, as a teacher, as a leader of the co-op, as a Christian. And in the collective nature of her assault, naming co-conspirators, I felt so very alone. I internalized her words in stunned silence. I didn't have a response. The cut was too deep and too near my heart.

JOY CLINE

Erich Brenn isn't a household name, but he made an appearance on television's *Ed Sullivan Show* in 1959.[3] Brenn earned his fame as a plate spinner. He would spin between ten to fifteen plates and bowls at a time, many atop poles, feverishly working to keep them all spinning at once without letting any of them stop or fall. It was an incredible feat dependent upon Brenn's constant attention and motion.

During this season of co-op and church, I felt every bit like Brenn, feverishly working to keep aloft and spinning the plates of *my* world—wife, mom, teacher, co-op co-administrator. It seemed, at the time, a daunting task, for my act wasn't four minutes long. It was ever ongoing. With that phone call, it was as if all that spinning had finally undone me and my plates all came crashing to the ground.

I hung up the phone and muddled my way through dinner somehow. Tonight was a dessert night at small group, so we had a little extra time to get out the door. I needed all the extra time I could get to compose myself for the night ahead. But by the time we got to the Bible study portion of the evening, my composure was cracking. Geoff likes to famously say that he can count on one hand the times he's seen me cry. I like to think it's that whole German reserve, though I'm sure he's also exaggerating a bit. I'd put the count closer to two hands. That night I simply came unglued. The retelling of the phone call came in bits and pieces as my sobs would allow. I just unleashed in the company of those who knew me well. I wept for the very real failure I felt as a wife, mom, teacher, and co-administrator. I wept for my perceived sense of harm to Daniel's classmates in our pursuit of inclusion. But mostly,

---

[3] *Erich Brenn - plate spinner*. Ed Sullivan Show. (2021, April 15). https://www.edsullivan.com/artists/erich-brenn-plate-spinner/

SPECIAL

I wept for my son and the seemingly impossible road before us littered with barbs.

In times like these, I count myself rich indeed to have a core group to surround me and lift me up when I can't do it myself. I know not everyone has such a luxury. That night my tears were finally stilled by my core who one by one spoke truth over me in words I could believe. Even better, they prayed over me…fervently.

And while by night's end nothing had changed…yet everything had changed. I was still battered and my confidence shaken, and we still hadn't a clue how we were going to navigate church and a life of such complexities with a special needs child. But what *had* changed was deep inside. My faith had been lifted and hope restored in their words and prayers over me. Perhaps even more importantly, my resolve had been reignited by the truth they poured into me to just keep battling.

We found our places where we could fit in at church, even thrive, mostly with the help of friends who stood in the gap for us. One of my friends who has a Down syndrome daughter, says it best, "My superpower is my friends." I think all of us raising special needs children can join in her sentiment. It was certainly true for us, especially at this stage of the journey.

One of these stalwarts was Ms. Tami. Ms. Tami led the charge for Faith Wranglers, Woodcrest's Wednesday evening children's program. Tami and I shared a friendship that extended beyond the walls of Woodcrest. We visited one another's home and saw ministry through much the same open-door lens. Ms. Tami made a place for Daniel at Faith Wranglers without the need of my ever-present shadow to integrate him, allowing me to serve in other capacities. Even more importantly, she resolutely defied anyone who might deny Daniel his equitable place there on Wednesday nights. She stood as one in authority where I, as a mom, could not, giving Daniel some of his first freedom to pursue his faith apart from us.

Another place at church where Daniel was able to exert his freedom was at Vacation Bible School. VBS, by nature, is a high energy week of summer fun, revolving around a theme and bringing the Bible to life. It was less academic, more drama-based in its approach, and loaded with games and food. Daniel loved it and greatly anticipated it each  summer. My role each week of VBS was to lead the opening and closing large group sessions, chipping in here and there in the in-between. As such, I had to rely on others to be with Daniel as he rotated through the assorted stations of his VBS day. Paula, as one of my core small group mates, intimately knew the struggle and didn't flinch. "Put Dan in my group!" she said. Paula didn't merely speak truth and pray over me in the moment of my deepest need, she followed it up with action.

Her willingness made all the difference for Daniel. For in the still, small moment near the end of VBS 2004, nine-year-old Daniel heard Ms. Ali's message about Jesus dying on the cross for his sins in a way that he could understand, and he asked Jesus to forgive him and come into his heart to be his Lord, Savior, and forever Friend.

In his disability, Daniel maybe didn't always "fit in" at church or in Christian circles, but there will *always* be room in God's kingdom. It has just taken a little time for the church to fling

SPECIAL

open its doors with the resources to support those with disabilities, but they're getting there. In the waiting, I was deeply grateful for people like Mrs. Doffing, Ms. Terri, Ms. Ali, Ms. Tami, and Paula, who rolled out the welcome mat to Jesus for Daniel.

6

WHAT'S *REALLY* IMPORTANT ANYWAY

One of the organizations that best engages and supports those with disabilities is Special Olympics. Special Olympics has been in existence now for nearly sixty years, providing spirited arenas of competition for Daniel and so many others like him. In fact, there are currently over 5.6 million Special Olympic athletes worldwide competing in over thirty individual and team sports.[4]

Admittedly, for how wonderful an organization Special Olympics is, my first brush with it brought an unusual emotion—resistance. I was still having a hard time coming to terms that Daniel actually belonged In such an arena, but here we were. Ten-year-old Daniel was competing in Special Olympics for the first time that spring of 2006, as part of the newly formed Farmington Tiger Paws delegation. It was a young delegation, consisting of athletes who were all yet in Farmington Public Schools. The delegation chose track and field for its first dabble into Special Olympics, and I remember well the team's first competition, the area qualifier at the White Bear Lake High School track.

As we shuttled Daniel to his various events, I was struck by the age of the participants I saw. In Farmington, we were decidedly on the younger end—the snacks and juice box sort, as I like

---

[4] *Special olympics*. SpecialOlympics.org. (n.d.). https://www.specialolympics.org/

SPECIAL

to say. This meet exposed me to athletes still participating into their 20s, 30s, 40s, 50s, 60s, 70s, and even 80s, with the oldest participants garnering some of the loudest applause for their grit and mettle. They looked a little disheveled and unkempt. Some made embarrassing noises and awkward comments. Few had supporters in tow to cheer them on. They represented a lifetime journey through Special Olympics I wasn't quite ready to embrace. It was as if I saw Daniel's future at that meet, and it sobered me in considering the endgame.

But as the meet wore on, it also grew on me. For while there were no snacks and juice boxes at this competition, there was an indomitable spirit—particularly amongst many of the older athletes who knew more of life and the struggles behind it—and it was infectious...whatever the age. It was in their shrieks of joy at winning. It was in their will to simply finish. And it was in their gestures of pure compassion for their fellow competitors' loss or pure delight in their victory. In their enthusiasm to compete, I found myself lifted and moved by the spirit of it all. My resistant heart softened.

Track and field became the go-to sport for the young Tiger Paws. It also became the platform for our most endearing Special Olympic moment. Daniel was now twelve years old and competing at the state games in the 200 meter dash, a race that included one of his Farmington teammates, Jacob.

Now I like to brand myself as one who applauds good sportsmanship and fine play—no matter the uniform. But if I'm to be honest, deep inside, I'm fiercely competitive. My family knows all too well that competitive streak that unleashes on Nebraska football Saturdays, in family games of Settlers of Catan, and at any sporting event my children are participating. And if you add into the mix a competitor who flaunts their superiority, it just amps up my competitive juices even more.

JOY CLINE

Such was the stage set for me that Saturday morning in June of 2008.

As Daniel was being readied for the race, our family spread out along the side of the University of Minnesota track at strategic positions, hoping to give Daniel the boost of encouragement he needed to run and to run fast. Geoff and Ben were along the turn, and Mary and I were at the homestretch. With a pop from the starter's gun, the runners were off. Daniel jumped out to a commanding lead, and I glowed at my son's athletic prowess. But as Daniel came down the stretch just past Mary and me along the fence line, I was mortified when he inexplicably stopped and ran in place ten feet from the finish line.

"Go, Daniel! Go! Go! GO!" I screamed, gold medal in sight. But Daniel just smiled and waved his teammate ahead of him so that Jacob crossed the finish line first and he finished second. I was stunned as we made our way over to the medals presentation. I watched from a distance, all the while snapping pictures and seething as Daniel was awarded the silver, while Jacob had the gold placed around his neck, much to the squeals of delight from his mother. Still disbelieving what I had just witnessed, we gathered around Daniel to admire his medal. Finally, with pleasantries aside, I could hold it in no longer, "Daniel, *why* did you stop and let Jacob win?"

"Because Jacob's my friend, and I wanted him to win," Daniel confided. And I realized in that moment with that simple

SPECIAL

answer that my special needs son got it, and I didn't. "Don't be selfish; don't try to impress others. Be humble, thinking of others as better than yourselves. Don't look out for your own interests, but take an interest in others, too."[5]

Apparently Geoff had the same lesson to learn as I did. For after two years of much the same results from Daniel, whether on the track or in the bowling alleys, Geoff decided it was time to instill a killer instinct in Daniel. So he upped the ante—big time—promising Daniel cable television if only he would run his hardest. The race was a bit longer—a 400, a full lap around the track. And once again, we spread out around the track to offer encouragement along the way. Daniel obliged, running the fastest I have ever seen him run. Whenever he began to lag, we piped up with the mantra: "Cable TV!" He ended up taking his race by a whopping 100 meters! He was a bit winded, but beaming. Who knew the motivating impact of unlimited *iCarly* television episodes?

Over the years, Daniel would go on to compete in many more Special Olympic sports: bowling, swimming, floor hockey,

basketball, and softball among them. The overriding benefit from all of these sports has been the relationships that have been forged along the way. It might be something as indescript as a chance meaningful interaction on the podium at the state swimming meet that one day would blossom into a best friendship. It might be the building of a team full of personalities that entertain us through a season of

---

[5] *Bible gateway passage: Philippians 2:3-4 - new international version.* Bible Gateway. (n.d.-j). https://www.biblegateway.com/passage/?search=Philippians+ 2%3A3-4&version=NIV

ups and downs, and twists and turns, taking us for a ride through predictable quirks and wonderful surprises. Such has been the case for us as Daniel has participated in floor hockey and softball over the years.

His floor hockey team epitomized that team full of personalities. There was Phillip, with his slow but deliberate approach to how and when he would play; Luna, with her sweet disposition and fiercer defense; Jake, with his pursuit of the puck that somehow found the nets; Maddie, with her quiet ways that came alive on the floor with her insistent stick tapping; Kane, with his bandanas and rocket slap shots; Sammy, with her shut-down defensive prowess and rallying cries that picked up the intensity; Aiden, with his strut and all the moves to the goal to back it up; and Daniel, with his knack for finding friendship in the nets.

Here in Minnesota, we take our hockey seriously, whether on the ice or in the gym. And as the team's goalie, Daniel was THE MAN. Never mind that he fielded pucks with his softball glove, the product of a small budget and lack of forethought into the possibility of a left-handed goalkeeper. Up in the stands, I lived the lonely life of a hockey goalie mom while

SPECIAL

Geoff helped coach. Games can be won or lost at goalie. As such, I watched most games as incognito as possible, praying for a good outcome. A few lapses in focus were all it took for scores to get quickly lopsided. While I was a mess watching, Daniel was pretty much unfazed no matter the result. Win or lose, his highlight was the congratulatory lineup at game's end.

Daniel's softball team had a few characters of its own. And with nine years under their belts together, their roles have become quite defined. There's Bobby, with his ever-present stuffed dog under arm that is "born ready" for everything thrown at him; Tom, with his nifty glove and helmet fetish; Jonda, with her perky personality that defies her forty-something age; Joe, with his late-arriving, big stick heroics; Addie, with her steady presence on the mound, as long as it's on her terms; Jake, with his understanding of the game that keeps everyone on their toes with his coaching; Klayton, with his called pitch counts and powerful arm; Sona, with her soft, whispery voice and powerful determination to compete; Jeff, with his burning speed few sixty-year olds possess; Sammy, with her impassioned cheers, hoping to cement the team together by sheer will; and Daniel, with his timely kind words to umpire and foe, diffusing high tensions with a smile.

Individually, they each have their strengths and weaknesses, but collectively they are the team we show up for every summer Tuesday night to marvel and applaud, and sometimes even grimace at their antics. Of course, there are nights when my competitive nature still gets the best of me. It might be in the showboating of a superior athlete or team, or in a pitcher's fast pitches in a slow pitch league, or in a close call in a tension-filled game. Whatever the case, whenever I feel myself caring a little too much, a voice reminds me what's *really* important anyways: "Jacob's my friend. I wanted him to win." Relationship rules.

7

WAYMAKER

If relationships rule, Daniel had the uncanny knack for finding them in some of the most unlikely places. It might be miles from home on a family vacation or steps from home in a local establishment. No matter the distance or novelty, all were fodder for Daniel's frolic and fun. He became, of sorts, our waymaker, opening doors closed by societal norms and enriching our lives through the interactions he backed us into.

The first opportunity we had to see this way-making knack was on our family trip to the East Coast in 2005. When the Clines do a family road trip, it must be understood that it will be long and the territory covered vast. Not only is the car packed to the gills, but the days as well. Relaxation is never part of the equation, only to see and to do. Our East Coast trip had stops in Washington DC, Rhode Island, Boston, Maine, the Berkshires, and Niagara Falls, and put 3,663 miles on our minivan. In order to afford family trips of such magnitude, we employed standby money-saving tactics: we all stayed in one room with double beds in hotels that were typically on the outskirts of cities, we made sure the hotel had a free breakfast and pool, we took full advantage of public transportation, and we only ate one meal out a day—often lunch, because it was cheaper than dinner.

Several days into our vacation, we were employing the tactics. We had taken the subway into DC from one of the outer ring suburbs, Springfield, which was the last stop on the blue

JOY CLINE

line. We arrived in DC after our hour commute with tickets in hand for a Capitol tour later that afternoon. With stomachs just beginning to growl, we prioritized lunch to ensure good attitudes on the tour. I had researched and found a nifty, but often untapped, restaurant in the basement of the Dirksen Senate Office Building. Besides being just a short walk to the Capitol, it also was known for being inexpensive and family friendly—a winning Cline combination! But family friendly can mean many things to many different people. In Daniel's mind, family friendly was all about the food and whether it was edible to his nine-year-old palate. And when it's your one meal out a day, the stakes can't get any higher. On Daniel's quick perusal of the offerings, they seemed to be lacking. He was dismayed, and he was hungry. Both feelings registered on his face. So when our waitress, a beautiful soul named Lorna, got around to taking Daniel's order, she read the situation perfectly.

"Not seeing anything you like, honey?" She ventured. "How about I go get you a grilled cheese sandwich. Would you like that?" And just like that, Daniel flashed her his big old smile, and she knew she had hit her mark. Lorna was a mom, and she got it. She kept close to our table the rest of lunch, and we were able to extract a little of her story and tips for navigating DC with kids. And when Geoff went to pay the bill, there wasn't a grilled cheese sandwich on it.

"It's on the house, honey." And Geoff flashed her *his* big old smile.

I'm not sure what it is about public transportation, but Daniel loves it and always has. Maybe it's the predictability of the stops, maybe it's the people watching, or maybe it's simply the drama and tensions afoot when traveling deep in the city. Whatever the case, he begs us, whenever possible, to forego the car in favor of light rail for a trip into Minneapolis.

SPECIAL

Fortunately, many of our family trips have afforded Daniel his public transportation fix. Such was the case on our Washington DC trip, as we became regulars on the blue line for the duration of our stay.

On one of our many ventures into the city, we settled into what was quickly becoming a familiar route, the stuff of which causes most commuters to close their eyes and bud up. Our train car was about half full of such commuters that morning, as few tourists travel into the city from such outer ring suburbs. As we perused our surroundings, one commuter in particular caught our attention, for he was decked from head to toe in military garb—not a typical sight for us Minnesotans far from home. He must have caught Daniel's attention as well. To our horror, the silence of the ride was shattered by his small innocent voice: "What are *you* doing?" By then, he had fortunately moved on from his standby, "What did you have for breakfast?"

The military man looked up from his early morning reverie, himself startled by the inquiry he had drawn. "I'm headed to work, buddy."

"Where do you work?"

"I work at the Pentagon. How about you? What are you doing?"

What ensued was a conversation initiated on uninhibited curiosity. It blossomed into a beautiful interaction we never, as adults, would have sought out on our own, stifled by societal constraints and conditioning that keep us in our own lanes. Reflecting back, I think what we would have missed had Daniel not been with us that day. We would have played it safe in our own contained world—silent, with eyes averted, content to mindlessly watch the familiar landscape pass us by. And in

JOY CLINE

so doing, simultaneously allowing opportunities to meet other people slip us by as well. In his insatiable quest for meaningful interactions, Daniel has always enlarged our world.

Such was the case days later when we traveled across Massachusetts to the Berkshires with tickets in hand for the Boston Pops. Mary and Ben were budding musicians in the Farmington schools at the time, and we thought exposure to the Boston Symphony Orchestra might light a fire to the spark they had already shown. As we drew nearer to Tanglewood, however, ominous clouds loomed on the horizon. We looked dismally at the fine print of our tickets for the show, which were, in fact, lawn tickets exposing us to the elements. On closer inspection, it seemed the show went on—rain or shine—as most of the higher-paying patrons sat comfortably under a large tent.

Ever the dad, Geoff swooped in to save the day by purchasing three large umbrellas before we headed out for the evening, sprinkles just beginning to fall. But we were not prepared for the deluge that greeted us as we arrived and that made a mockery of our umbrellas. Even the ticket-taker eyed us incredulously as she reminded us that our tickets were only for sitting on the lawn beyond the tent—the same lawn that now fielded numerous and deep puddles, and was anything but habitable with blankets. The show's start bearing down on us, we were in a quandary. We stood in the aisle at the tent's edge, just out of reach of the cascading drips.

Daniel must have grown tired of standing and listening to all our strategizing, and had plopped himself down on a corner of the last row of protected bench seating. Our lawn ticket gamble all but hopeless, we decided to cut our losses and head back to the hotel. But when we went to gather Daniel, we found him already engaged in a conversation with an

SPECIAL

elderly woman he had sat down beside. Her name, we were to find, was Rosemarie, and she had traveled from Long Island with a group of her friends as part of a tour group attending the concert that night. Our connection deepened as we discovered we shared the same hotel in the Berkshires. Greater still, we found in Rosemarie a stalwart advocate. The clock ticking, she took charge, rallying her "girls" and those around them to scootch together to make room for our kids, who squeezed in amongst them. A sympathizing usher allowed Geoff and me to stand behind the last bench within a whisker of the cascade. While Geoff had swept in to save our evening with his purchase of the umbrellas that were no match for the rain we encountered, the true heroine of the night was Rosemarie, who turned our evening from disaster to delight, made all the more memorable for the connection made.

But we were to find Daniel's knack for way-making extended far beyond the confines of our family vacations. It happened in the ordinary, the everyday. When we went to Pellicci's Ace Hardware, Stu was quick to fill a bag of popcorn for Daniel. He knew food, and especially popcorn, was the way to Daniel's heart. Was it any wonder that Daniel was quick to tag along for any and all hardware visits? Kwik Trip Cathy bellowed a hearty, "Hi Danny!" whenever we entered the store for bags of milk. The same greeting chased us down from the outdoor loudspeakers whenever we were pumping gas or walking the dog past Kwik Trip. Daniel simply beamed in the attention of it all. Trevor from Farmington Eye Clinic indulged Daniel in allowing him to call him "Howie," a nod to Trevor's uncanny

JOY CLINE

resemblance to Howie Mandel of *America's Got Talent*. When I was pressed for time and attempting to dash through my grocery list, Daniel couldn't bypass Steve the Doritos guy in the aisles of Cub Foods. Even as I was trying to tug him back on task so I could complete my list, he heralded Steve, who never tired of engaging Daniel in a conversation about the weather. Daniel always had a higher calling that seemed to supersede my ever present "to do" lists.

In his innocence, Daniel was the vehicle through which our lives intersected with those we never could have imagined, and our lives were broadened and enriched because of it. The common denominator was that all had a soft spot for Daniel and never tired of making him feel special and valued. If there's one thing we've learned through the years, it's that some people have that ability, while others do not. We tend to be friends with those that do.

8

A FAMILY AFFAIR

W hile we surrounded ourselves with friends who embraced and championed Daniel, as siblings, Mary and Ben had no choice in the matter. They were born into our family and had to figure it out. Having a brother with special needs became the classroom from which they were ever learning and growing and being challenged. Sometimes they basked in the notoriety of Daniel, while other times they wanted to distance themselves from him. At times they were his ardent defenders, while at other times they found him easy pickings for their own manipulative schemes. Their reality was that he made their lives different, and all this at an age when they were forever trying to fit in—particularly as homeschoolers.

One word to describe Mary and Daniel's relationship growing up: complicated. Daniel fairly worshiped the ground Mary walked on. She parlayed this influence over Daniel, amping him up in situations and garnering his support for her higher plans. It might be as simple as winning her choice of movie for family movie night or as detrimental as derailing a family trip. Together they were a formidable force. So much so, we called them Thunder and Lightning. They reacted off one another and carried a big boom. As the eldest child, Mary held the psychological edge and used it to her full advantage. Whenever she wanted to create a little stirring or mount a defense against Dad and Mom, Daniel was her ready ally. She had only to suggest, and he fell in line behind her.

For his part, Daniel reveled in the camaraderie of Mary. He was a willing participant in her schemes. In her company, he elevated his third child status. Both benefited from this alliance, until they didn't any longer. It then often spiraled into Daniel mimicking Mary's words or actions, and Mary seeking justice from an annoying brother. They both knew how to push one another's buttons and did so incessantly.

Ben and Daniel were closest in age and shared a bedroom together in the early years. In Daniel, Ben found a ready playmate in a neighborhood with few options. It might be cards, Boccerball, or some made up game on the trampoline. Whatever the activity, Ben had an inbuilt competition of his own design. Daniel, of course, was the insurance for Ben that he would win every game played. It was an arrangement that satisfied them both—Ben in his competitive nature and Daniel in his sense of belonging.

One Cline family game we had when riding in the car was the bridge game. Whenever we crossed a bridge, you held your breath for the duration. Mary, Ben, and Daniel would inhale deeply at bridge's start and let out an exaggerated exhale at bridge's end. The louder the exhale, the longer the bridge. Rule follower that he was, Ben adhered to the game's parameters. The Mendota Bridge was the tantamount test; and in its length, Ben's small lungs were no match. He exhaled before bridge's

SPECIAL

end, gasping for his breath while peering at the competition. One look at Daniel, cheeks puffed and nostrils flaring before issuing a long, satisfied exhale at bridge's end, unhinged him.

"Daniel's cheating!" Ben cried in virtuous protest. "He's breathing through his nose. No fair!"

Score one for the little brother.

We saw all these relational dynamics come into full display on our long road trips. There's nothing like twelve hours together in the close confines of a car to expose fissures in the family facade. On one particular family vacation, we were on our way to tour George Washington's Mount Vernon estate. As we drew ever closer, a sign signaled a ferry landing on the Potomac River that ran parallel to the estate. The sign sparked a memory for me from a historical fiction we had read for homeschooling about the early life of our first President. Ever the teacher, I pounced on it as a teachable moment.

"Hey guys, do you remember that book we read about George Washington and his cousin Patty? Here's probably the ferry landing where Patty got her pony."

"Who's Patty?" asked Mary.

"You know…George Washington's cousin…the one who used to visit him. Remember? She waited at the ferry landing for the boat coming to bring her pony." They looked at me with blank stares. "You know…Patty," I offered, a little less enthusiastically. In the deafening silence and with my credibility as a teacher on the line, I began fuming, incredulous they didn't remember this book as well as I did. Then a still, small voice broke the silence.

JOY CLINE

"Who's Patty?" Daniel asked innocently, taking cues from Mary and looking to her for encouragement. And with that, a chorus of "Who's Patty?" rang out in the van.

They knew they had met my tipping point. The rest of the day soured from there, as Geoff sided with me to even the divide. Ben, ever the middle child, remained silent and noncommittal. The next day dawned no brighter as Mary and Daniel fell into giggling and chirping, "Who's Patty?" at strategic, stress-filled moments of the day. It took threats of Georgie, Daniel's beloved stuffed green gorilla, being tossed out the window and a ninety-minute layover at a Connecticut wayside rest that delayed our Rhode Island beach day until Mary and Daniel could apologize. Real family moments...at least I can celebrate as their teacher that they weren't asking, "Who's George Washington?"

Weeks after returning from our East Coast trip, I was cleaning out the van of its remnants when I came across a tightly folded scrap of paper. Curious, I carefully unfolded its tattered remains to reveal Ben's scrawling script: "I hate tension."

Despite our best efforts, tension did, at times, enter our home as we tried to balance avoiding Daniel's meltdowns with maintaining a sense of fairness and justice for all. When we turned a blind eye and tilted towards keeping the peace, Mary and Ben protested the double standards for behaviors they would not be allowed to get away with. When we upheld family rules judiciously, we risked drawing battle lines in the sand with Daniel. He was never very fond of battle lines without exit strategies. Our day could deteriorate quickly. We were ever reworking our disciplinary compass as we figured out what worked and what didn't work with Daniel. There was no manual for these family dynamics. It was all on-the-job training.

SPECIAL

And the training was not uniquely ours as parents. Due to our social connections and commitments, Mary and Ben were often forced into the parental role at small group, play dates, church, and co-op gatherings when the kids all went off to play together. Though kids themselves, they had the added responsibility of being their brother's keeper—or maybe better said, their brother's keeper-in-line. Much was expected of them as siblings of a special needs brother. They were faced with the same balancing act as Geoff and I, as they tried to set Daniel up for success so they might have a little fun themselves. Sometimes it was just too much for them, as Ben once lamented in exasperation, "I wish I had a normal brother."

But time and maturity are great expanders of perspective. Though once expected to care for his brother, Ben *chose* to spend his senior year homeroom class volunteering in Daniel's special education classroom. He played UNO and other games with the students, and received so much more in return as they fairly bowled him over with their affection. Working with special needs students has a way of shifting your gaze from what *you* think is important to what really *is* important. I believe those homeroom classes altered Ben's understanding of his brother. So much so that as Ben contemplated his honor's thesis in college, he focused on Daniel, exploring an idea at the intersection of his dual philosophy/psychology majors and faith. The gist of it questioned Daniel's "need" for healing. Most would say Daniel would be better off if God healed him of his disability, but Ben wrestled with healing's impact on those characteristics of Daniel he most admired—his genuineness, purity of heart, and unabashed joy. Is that really a "healing?" We have come across many well-meaning people across life who wanted to pray for just that—Daniel's healing. It has always left us uncomfortable because we, too, wrestle with Ben's paradox. We have come to the conclusion that we think Daniel's pretty special just the way he is.

JOY CLINE

As Mary transitioned from high school into college, she was on a journey of her own. She knew she wanted to be a teacher of young children, but was unsure of what licensure to pursue. My brother Joey, a principal at a local elementary school, stepped in to offer some advice for navigating what then was a competitive job market for teachers. He suggested she diversify and pair her elementary education degree with another, such as special education, a language, or English as a Second Language (ESL). Mary was quick to rule out special education. "I've lived it my whole life," she quipped. "I don't want to make it my job as well."

I know some teachers are called into special education *because* of a sibling with special needs. Mary was not one of those, and I'm proud of her for recognizing that in herself. She chose, instead, to be an ESL teacher at the elementary level. And while not working with special education students all hours of her day, Mary is every bit the compassionate, empathetic champion of the special education students she does have. And to this day, Mary can still—with a twinkle in her eyes and an inflection to her voice—get Daniel right there with her. Watch out, world!

On October 13, 2018, Ben married the love of his life, Allison. And with that union, Daniel gained yet another sibling. Allison came into our family as one untarnished by the past history of a shared childhood. From early on she had an ease and natural connection with Daniel. We saw it in the ways she was able to gain his trust and make him laugh. Like with his sister Mary, Daniel adored Allison.

As Allison's relationship with Ben deepened and she spent more time with our family, she also became intuitive to Daniel's struggles, seeking to shield or grow him. She invited Daniel into her love of horses by taking him along to ride her old horse, Trigger. Daniel was a bit apprehensive and hesitant to even approach Trigger. But with Allison's coaxing and encouragement, his confidence grew that day.

For our part, if the heart quotient towards Daniel is a measuring stick for our closest friendships, imagine the inspection Allison unknowingly endured as one possibly joining our family. Ben didn't need to worry…she not only passed our judgment, but also won our hearts. We even took to telling him he "better not mess this up." Fair warning, anyone coming knocking for Mary's hand in marriage will undergo the same scrutiny.

Daniel is an incredible judge of character. Allison goes toe-to-toe with him in that regard; and in Daniel, she saw one who was without pretense, kind, and pure of heart. Apparently Daniel's stuffed gorilla, Georgie, shares that same ability, for he was alongside Daniel, adorned in a top hat, as Daniel toasted Ben and Allison at their groom's dinner the night before their wedding.

"Allison is just like Ben. She knew riding a horse would be a scary thing, so she helped it to be easier for me. She even came to visit me at Bethel and had lunch with me. Georgie's with me tonight…all dressed up for Ben and Allison's wedding. I love you, Ben. You have always cared for me and looked out for me. I'm excited to have Allison as my new sister. She has a heart like you. I think Georgie will love her too."

JOY CLINE

It was a fitting welcome into our family, as only Daniel could pull off. Allison must have thought so too, as she wiped away tears as Daniel wrapped his arms around her in an embrace.

9

VULNERABILITIES

We all experience vulnerability as we confront varying situations in our lives. It's a rite of passage. However, for those with special needs, those vulnerabilities are often more numerous and may linger a lifetime. As parents of special needs children, we are ever wary and measuring of our environment. We identify situational minefields and establish safeguards to protect them. It can, at times, be a daunting game of Whack-a-Mole, because you can never cover everything. It is in those times I am reduced to a simple prayer voiced in utter resignation, "Lord, I can't be with Daniel right now, but I know You are. Protect him. Keep him safe. I give him to Your sovereign care. You are good. You are trustworthy. Amen."

As Daniel aged, his vulnerabilities became more pronounced. The one that superseded all others for him was trust. Daniel had an inherent trust in the good nature of others. If someone saw his lunch and thought it looked better than his own, he only needed to ask and Daniel would give it to him. If another needed a phone for a call, Daniel was his guy. If someone eyed Daniel's spot in line, Daniel was quick to go to the back. Simple stuff.

And while we taught Daniel to trust in God and in others, we were increasingly living in a world where you could no longer trust in the genuine good nature of others. And that's when the simple stuff became more complex. We saw it in the question of whether to send Daniel to youth group at church. While

JOY CLINE

church is typically a safe place, ours had a seeker-friendly vibe on Wednesday nights. The music was loud, the lights were low, the crowd was vast, and it all attracted an audience of whom all weren't necessarily there for Jesus. It was an incredibly hard unspoken message to convey to Daniel that he wasn't "safe" at church. His trust issues kept him home with us on Wednesday nights, even as his sister and brother headed out the door. There's a limit to being your brother's keeper.

Even our neighborhood, small as it was at only two blocks long, posed unsafe for Daniel's vulnerabilities. Next door to us lived Tim. Tim was a mentally unstable, thirty-something, who was out of work and living with his grandma and mom. Tim loved cigarettes, rap music, and the Boston Celtics. He also loved spending time with Daniel, some twenty years his junior. He would come over asking if Daniel could play hoops in our driveway and serenade him with "Danny Boy." He wrote letters to him.

As Tim's mental state deteriorated, we became fearful of his capabilities. Tim was a big man. After one family altercation, Geoff warned his mom and grandma that they should seek outside help or they might become victims. In the meantime, we wrestled with what to do with Daniel. He struggled to see Tim as a threat, this man who belted out "Danny Boy" and brought a smile to his face. And didn't Jesus command us to "love our neighbor as ourselves?"[6] For Daniel, who knew Jesus' words implicitly, their literal interpretation proved a stumbling block.

At the time, Daniel was in high school, still catching a bus in the morning. He often left the house about twenty minutes

---

[6] *Bible gateway passage: Mark 12:30-31 - new international version.* Bible Gateway. (n.d.). https://www.biblegateway.com/passage/?search=Mark+12%3A30 -31&version=NIV

SPECIAL

after I did, leaving an unaccounted gap. As much as we could plead with Daniel to stay inside and look for the bus from our living room bay window, there was no assurance what he might do if Tim came knocking and we weren't there.

One day a brooding Tim walked up and down the street with a pitchfork slung over his shoulder...and not for gardening. It was an image of instability, and it was the last straw. Geoff made a second trip next door, but this time he made the hard request that Tim not have any contact with Daniel. Months later, Tim murdered his grandma with a hammer as she slept. Her bedroom was literally feet from our house where Daniel had a friend spending the night for MEA weekend. We shuddered to think what might have happened if Daniel had crossed paths with Tim that fateful night, under the state of mind that he was in. Even we failed to grasp the scope and scale of Tim's mental instability, and our oversight scared us.

Yet this failure to rightfully size up a situation had surfaced years earlier. You think we would have learned. It came on a most perfect of May evenings, when it seemed nothing could be amiss with the world. We had attended church earlier that evening at River Valley Church in Apple Valley and headed afterwards to small group at some friends' home nearby. We now were at a new church and in a new small group, yet these new relationships had solidified quickly. Daniel was fourteen at the time and planned on hanging out with the rest of the kids as the parents met for Bible study. Mary and Ben, now in high school, no longer came along with us to small group.

As the adults settled in for our time together, the kids decided to take advantage of the unseasonably warm spring evening for a friendly game of hide and seek. Before long, they began trickling in from outdoors, their empty stomachs luring them to the spread of treats that signaled the meeting's end. I kept looking for Daniel with each wave of kids. Not seeing him, I got up to check the rest of the house.

"Jake, do you know where Daniel is?" I asked the boy in charge of the evening's fun.

"He was with Celia."

"But Celia's right here, and Daniel isn't anywhere." Jake shrugged, and anxiety started to mount. I returned to our small group. "Hey, guys, I can't find Daniel anywhere. He didn't come back in with the rest."

After questioning the kids on their last sighting of Daniel, we spread out into the neighborhood, calling out for Daniel. At first our circle remained small and contained. But with the deafening silence in return to our calls, we ventured farther and farther out. Dusk was beginning to fall, and the twisty-turny nature of the large suburban neighborhood had us turned all around. I found myself repeatedly circling back to the same spot. In my confusion, I tried to keep my bearing, while worrying how Daniel was navigating this same strange and looping neighborhood. My fears dug in a little deeper. By now, some of the neighbors had heard of Daniel's demise and had picked up the charge.

With darkness quickly descending and with it much cooler temperatures, we realized our window of opportunity to find Daniel was narrowing. I just kept thinking how so very scared he must be all alone in the unfamiliar and dark. I called Mary and Ben to come and help us with the search, while Geoff notified the local police. It wasn't long before we began to see squad cars scouring the area. At one point in my search, I came upon a nearby park where an officer on foot was shining a bright searchlight across the surface of a pond.

SPECIAL

The gravity of our situation fully descended on me. I realized the larger implications of danger for a lost child wandering unaccompanied. I knew back at the house there were those left behind who were praying for Daniel. My job was to keep calling and searching, even as I cried out to God in bursts to find my boy. I was now the scared one, and a whole new set of "what-if's" were chasing me down as Daniel remained unaccounted for.

One who also hadn't abandoned the search was Jeff Thommes, one of our small group friends. Jeff was the quintessential outdoorsman. Every season, in his mind, was one in pursuit of game or fish. In fact, when the small group Ice Breaker question was posed about our favorite season, Jeff immediately quipped, "Hunting!" Seasoned outdoorsman that he was, Jeff had an acute eye for detail and tracking. In his hunt for Daniel, he had strayed to the far edge of the neighborhood, when something caught his eye. Plastered to the cement sidewalk was a name tag from River Valley's Go Kids program bearing Celia's name. Knowing Daniel and Celia had been together earlier in the evening, Jeff surmised he might be on the right trail and ventured a little farther. It wasn't long before he spotted someone in the distance whom he thought was Daniel.

"Hey, Daniel, is that you? It's Jeff Thommes."

"Yes" was Daniel's understated reply.

"Hey, we've been looking all over for you, buddy," said Jeff. "Come on, let's get you back to the Kiley's. I know your mom and dad will be really excited to see you."

As Jeff made small talk, he said Daniel didn't talk much on the nine-block walk back to small group. In fact, we were

JOY CLINE

never able to get much at all out of him about his ordeal. The snippets we did get were that he had walked much farther than we had thought possible, finding familiar major roads to gather his bearings. At one point, Daniel even said he walked past our church. He never was able to fully articulate his journey or his fears. To this day, he holds his emotions close to his cuff, a product of his autism. We were left to imagine the gaps.

Word got back that Jeff had Daniel, and the police were called off the search. Everyone had gathered back at the house for Daniel's arrival, mobbing and hugging him when he got back to the Kiley's. For his part, Daniel seemed overwhelmed by the fuss. He just wanted to get some treats and plop in front of the TV with the rest of the kids. Days later, seven-year-old Kaitlyn would recount the night in a story she wrote at school. But like us, the ending baffled her. "And then he just came and sat on the couch and watched a movie," she wrote. "That was weird."

That brush with danger, however "weird," jolted Geoff and me out of a complacency we had settled into as Daniel grew older and more independent. We recognized within it our failure to account for an unfamiliar environment for Daniel or to provide him with the tools to navigate it. As trusting as Daniel typically was, stranger danger kept him paralyzed from seeking help that night. Even if he had sought aid at a neighbor's door, we realized he didn't know our cell phone numbers by heart, nor did he have his own phone, as cell phones were a recent addition to our lives. We had set Daniel up for failure in our lapse, and it sobered us as few events in life ever have.

While we could learn and grow with certain of Daniel's vulnerabilities, one in particular defied our ability to contain or control: his health. That said, Daniel was a relatively healthy boy. He rarely got sick; and when he did, it was mostly short-lived and of the common nature. One recurring "illness" Daniel

SPECIAL

experienced that has since disappeared, left us baffled for years. It typically came on as we were all sitting around the table having dinner—coincidentally, often when we were eating chicken. The first sign was that we would notice Daniel eating really slowly, picking at his food. Then he'd grow strangely quiet, the color draining from his face. Daniel not eating and quiet? Definitely something is not right!

"Are you okay, Daniel?"

"I'm fine," he'd respond, his voice laced with agitation.

Within moments, his cheeks would puff and he'd go racing for the toilet, where he would throw up all of his dinner, several times over. He'd continue to vomit the rest of the evening before retiring to bed far earlier than what was typical for him. Yet in the morning he would awaken with appetite and words restored, and we would quickly dismiss the night's drama and move on…until the next time. Though with each episode and its loose connection to chicken, Daniel became leery each time chicken was on the menu.

Within all of this, we realized another alarming pattern was starting to emerge. Daniel never let us know when he wasn't feeling well. In fact, he'd go to great lengths to disguise and vehemently deny it. Often Geoff and I were left to our own instincts to recognize symptoms and step in. In Daniel's silence, we were ever playing the role of mind readers, hoping we got it right.

Most of the time, though, his silence was inconsequential. Beyond the seasonal coughs and sniffles, we were lulled into complacency by Daniel's healthiness—a complacency that would be rattled by a threatening and unexplained illness that seemed to come out of nowhere. It happened the Saturday

JOY CLINE

before Daniel was to start seventh grade at Farmington Middle School East. We were doing the normal stuff of a Saturday afternoon, when Daniel was struck by a debilitating headache and extreme dizziness. His eyes were unable to focus, and he just closed them and laid his head back and moaned. As I peppered him with questions he was unable to answer, I knew he was about to lose it...literally. I dashed to grab a bowl, and he proceeded to throw up over and over and over again.

By then Geoff had come into the house and realized all was not right. As parents facing an emergency, you are left to quickly assess and make your best call. In that it was a Saturday, we had two options to get Daniel some help: Urgent Care or the hospital emergency room. We opted for the closer, Urgent Care, hoping to get Daniel some relief as quickly as possible in a setting that wouldn't be quite so scary. We managed to get him to the car and raced off for the nearest Urgent Care some fifteen minutes away. In route, we tried to gather from Daniel the circumstances that led to the onset of his sudden sickness. We asked questions of where he was feeling pain. Mostly, our questions were met with moans, with a few *yes's* and *no's* sprinkled in, seemingly to satisfy and quiet us. Geoff drove a little faster.

We got to the Urgent Care and helped Daniel into the reception room, thankful to find it wasn't overflowing—probably due to the time of year and that it was Labor Day weekend. We were ushered to the back in no time, Daniel holding his ever-present bowl. The doctor on duty took his vitals and asked us lots of questions, for most of which we didn't have any definitive answers. Daniel certainly had none. The doctor took another look at Daniel and said, "I don't have much I can do for him. You need to take him to the emergency room...now."

If there was a sense of urgency before, it was even more heightened now. Geoff drove even faster with red lights and

SPECIAL

stop signs along the way becoming optional for our twenty-five minute drive to Children's Hospital in St. Paul. Daniel was still throwing up—a blessing in disguise, as they were quick to get him out of the waiting room and into an evaluation room.

Once there, vitals were again gathered and the questions commenced: When did this start? What hurts? Did you get hit in the head? The last one gave us pause...*did Daniel somehow hit his head?* We traced back the events of the day, trying to pinpoint a scenario where he might have taken a blow to the head: Did you fall down? Did you hit your head on the bed? Did a ball hit you? Did the milk crates at Kwik Trip fall on you? We were reaching, and Daniel's inconsistent responses weren't helping. The doctor was quick to jump on his inconsistencies, and pretty soon we sensed a shift in the questioning that put the spotlight on us as parents with an accusatory undercurrent of abuse. Daniel's inability or reluctance to articulate was costing us our credibility.

As they began the litany of tests that we hoped would identify the cause of Daniel's malaise, the Lord lightened our hearts with His providential positioning. Walking into our room that evening was Kristin, a pediatric physician's assistant. Even better, Kristin was one of our stalwarts from our family small group at Woodcrest. Kristin knew us, and she knew us well. Ours was a relationship chiseled from years of doing life in the trenches together on those small group Friday nights, and this was a very trench-like moment. Her very presence that night for our shared history steadied us as if the Lord Himself were present. She was that familiar face of comfort for Daniel when he needed it most.

"Hey buddy, how are ya doing?" Kristin asked, with a tenderness that spoke of familiarity.

JOY CLINE

"Good," replied a weakened Daniel, giving his pat answer he would reply in even the most dire of situations.

"I'm so sorry you're feeling so crummy. I know this isn't fun. Is there anything I can get you? A blanket? Some water? Would you like me to turn on the TV?" With a nod of his head, she flicked the TV on and found a channel to his liking to distract him.

Kristin was able to meet us in the moment as both a physician and a friend. We were able to share with her in unguarded words all that had happened that day, and she just hugged us and cried with us. It was what we needed.

Tears in her eyes, Kristin gave Daniel's hand one last squeeze. "I told them I was going to have to sequester myself from this patient. It's just too close to me, but I made sure you'll get the best of care." And with that, she left us, but her presence lingered for the peace God gave us through her.

All told, our emergency room visit lasted six hours before they were able to run a full battery of tests and imagings, and get their results. In the meantime, they were able to finally stabilize Daniel with medication and fluids enough to be released. As for all the tests, they proved inconclusive for determining what caused this sudden malady. We left the hospital late that night with nearly as many questions as we had that afternoon when we arrived.

And while we were deeply thankful to have this behind us and our boy back to his old cheerful self, the lack of answers left us with a nagging fear of fragility hanging over Daniel. We would see this demise raise its ugly head two more times in his life—never as severe as his first bout, but just as scary in its suddenness and unpredictability.

10

A DIFFERENT KIND OF EDUCATION

Daniel's inaugural middle school IEP meeting was a wake-up call for us. Though he seemingly headed off to school happy enough, we were unaware of the distress he was under. The IEP—the same one that reduced me to tears—shed light on Daniel's days, even as he could not—or would not—divulge the details.

Middle school is a powder keg of energy, drama, hormones, and newfound independence. Daniel, new to this whole thing of being in school all day, found himself solidly in the throws of it all. He wanted so much to integrate into its culture, but couldn't always figure out how to do so. Daniel's default, as always, was to mimic. If someone got a laugh in class because of something they said, Daniel was quick to parrot it. If someone sneezed loudly to elicit a "bless you," Daniel followed with his own exaggerated sneeze. Even if someone tripped and dropped their books, Daniel would giggle, hit the ground, and feign the same. He needed coaching to be compassionate of others' mishaps. As for his classmates, they found this all annoying. And what Daniel hoped might endear him to the rest of the class, actually resulted in him being shunned.

It was into this world that I boldly forged when I signed up to chaperone one of Daniel's school field trips. By then I was only

JOY CLINE

homeschooling Ben, and my days were suddenly a bit more open. Besides, I was excited to spend the day with Daniel and have an eye into his newfound middle school environs. He and around a hundred of his classmates were headed to the River Rendezvous at the Pond Dakota Mission Park in nearby Bloomington on that autumn day. River Rendezvous, nestled on the shores of the Minnesota River, is a historic re-enactment of the life and work of nineteenth century Native Americans and pioneers. Student groups rotate to different stations to interact with costumed presenters, learning trades of the times and participating in assorted tasks from fur tanning, to blacksmithing, to coopering, to laundering.

Our group was so large that we split up into four smaller ones, leaving me to shadow Daniel's group. Together we shuffled from presenter to presenter, learning the ways of the past. At one stop, we listened to a Native American man share about his cultural artifacts. As he was speaking, a movement drew my attention as one of our students was circling around the outside of the group for a better view. Austin dodged in and out until he settled on a spot just behind Daniel. As my eyes shifted back to the presentation, I just glimpsed Austin giving Daniel a shove that toppled him into the students in front of him, who squirmed uncomfortably. It was not an accidental nudge, but a full throttle shove that took Daniel by surprise. It took me by surprise as well. Not wanting to interrupt the speaker in his sharing, I glared at Austin from afar. He caught my gaze as it bored into him, and looked away. Afterwards, I caught up to him and locked step with him.

"Hey, Austin, why'd you shove Daniel?"

"I dunno." And he trotted ahead to join a group of his friends. I weighed whether to pursue him further and decided to back

SPECIAL

off. I quickly assessed this was a no-win situation—for Daniel or for me.

But things didn't get better for Daniel that day. Later, I caught Daniel talking with a couple of girls. Daniel always preferred the company of girls in these situations. I think they made him feel safer. Daniel must have said or done something wrong though, because the next thing I heard was one of the girls exclaiming in a tired voice, "Dan-iel!" Then they turned and walked away from him, giggling all the way. My heart ached for my boy in the cruelty of it all.

These were the situations I stumbled upon that day, but what were the ones I didn't see? And were all of his days like this?

Middle school can be vicious as students jostle for positions and social groups. In all of this, Daniel was easy pickings in his yielding nature. He was decidedly on the bottom rung. Yet even as he was the one to be picked on and blamed by his classmates, the hallways between classes became his domain. It was in the hallways where he shined. Unaccompanied by an aide, he was able to drift between classes fitting in as many positive interactions as possible. While the social interactions of the classroom befuddled him, he knew and understood the social dynamics of the hallways. He'd greet everyone with a "hey," give a wave of his hand, and flash a big old smile. His friendliness was infectious. Others returned his greetings, particularly seventh graders, who were untainted by the Daniel of the classroom. They only saw the Daniel of the hallway, and they kind of liked him.

That year's IEP also instituted a major shift in how the school district serviced his disability. It was in that meeting it became clear that Daniel's greater struggles were of the cognitive nature, instead of his autism. The school staff recommended

JOY CLINE

he still receive some ASD services, but primarily be housed in the DCD classroom. So though he began his middle school days in the autism classroom, he ended them in the DCD classroom. Besides the classroom shift, there was also a district-wide building shift that displaced Daniel to an entirely different school for his eighth grade year. It was a lot of change for one for whom change is hard.

But while change can be hard, not all change is bad. At Boeckman Middle School, Daniel had a new teacher with a clear, defined routine. Daniel always thrived with routine. It seemed a safe place for him, and he flourished. By then, the prevailing winds brought a new collection of classmates to Daniel's days who seemed more empathetic. Whether a change of scenery or a boost in maturity, Daniel was beginning to figure out this whole middle school thing...just as it was coming to an end.

The end of the school year is marked by a dizzying series of lasts—the last field trip, the last sporting event, the last band concert, the last day. For Daniel, his big "last" circled prominently on the family calendar was his last choir concert. Daniel has always loved music, an extension of having a musical sister and brother. He's been a devoted viewer of shows like *The Voice, American Idol,* and *America's Got Talent.* To this day, he will burst out in song on a whim and regularly serenade us from the bathroom. It was no surprise, then, when he chose choir as his elective class in eighth grade. Daniel's favorite hour of the day was choir, when he got to escape from the confines of the DCD classroom and join his mainstream classmates in the choir room. He always preferred the inclusive classes over his special ed ones. Choir afforded him a fenceless pasture from which he could roam and grow socially.

SPECIAL

The last choir concerts of the year in Farmington typically highlight multi-voiced and choreographed numbers. They are a chance for students to show off the skills of a year's worth of labor. Daniel was so excited that night to finally be the Cline up on the stage and not the one in the audience. He didn't even mind the jeans he needed to wear as part of his costume. Daniel has mostly eschewed jeans, preferring sweats instead because of how they feel against his skin, a trait of his autism's tactile sensitivity.

Watching from the auditorium seats at that last concert, I marveled at the growth I saw in Daniel. This boy for whom communication had always been difficult was up there on the stage singing his heart out. He knew the words! When it came time for hand gestures, he was a picture of focus and concentration as he tried to keep pace with his classmates, ever eyeing them for cues to the next move. He often was about a second behind the others, but he was doing it! The ultimate test came on the last song, when the choir ditched the risers for the stage itself and added some dance moves. This was a high task for Daniel, and it showed. He didn't always know whether he was coming or going, but he thrilled for it the same—a big smile radiated his joy of being in the moment.

As Daniel attempted to keep up with his classmates, we noticed one boy in particular, who seemed tasked with helping orient Daniel. He would point to him where to go, and lead him when he needed additional assistance. It was a tender moment for me to behold here at middle school's end for the journey of it all. But something seemed familiar about this boy. I studied his features more intensely and saw in him the unmistakable recognition. It was Austin—that same Austin of shoving renown from a couple of years earlier! And my heart swelled even more. Austin's gesture spoke of a symbolic shift

JOY CLINE

of acceptance for us amongst Daniel's classmates. No longer was he the maligned one. Slowly but surely, the Unsinkable Daniel Cline was beginning to rise, just in time for his debut into the high school scene in the fall.

11

RISING

Daniel entered Farmington High School in the fall of 2010, just a year after it had opened the doors to its new, state-of-the-art facility. It was an exciting time, and Daniel was energized by the even greater freedoms high school afforded. The hallways remained his domain where he could fit in all the interactions possible in a four-minute passing and still get to class on time. He had it down to the second.

By now, Daniel was making a name for himself. It certainly helped that for the first time in Cline family history, all three Cline children were under the same school roof. Mary was just beginning her senior year, while Ben was a junior. Daniel benefited from the name recognition of his older siblings and the trail they blazed for him.

Besides all three kids roaming the halls, I also spent about three days a week substitute teaching at FHS. Unfortunately

JOY CLINE

for the Cline kids, they were never far from my watchful gaze or straining ears. I had each of them in my class with some frequency, as I seemed to be a regular for many of their teachers. It was a little awkward, and we all grew used to the snickers as I read off their names for attendance. They certainly felt the weight of accountability by having me in the building, but I also think they kind of liked knowing they could track me down across their school days if anything came up.

Despite the pristine new school feel and all the family vibes contained within it, all was not perfect for Daniel. His vulnerabilities still chased him down from time to time. For his trusting nature, Daniel was particularly unguarded with those he knew and with whom he desired friendship. One day in the cafeteria, a group of older girls he knew called him over to their table. Daniel was quick to oblige. Sadly, it wasn't every day a DCD student was asked to join the tables of the larger student population, and Daniel was giddy at the opportunity. Phones in hand, the girls chatted away with him. Cell phones were a recent addition to the campus landscape. Students were engrossed in the novelty of them, while administrators played catch up, trying to determine how to best coexist with them.

In time, however, the chatter evolved into one of the girls, Sara, hitting the record button on her phone, as the others urged Daniel to do silly, embarrassing things. The girls found they only needed to ask Daniel, and he willingly did their bidding. It seemed innocent enough…until it wasn't any longer. The share button was tapped, and the video found its way circulating across phones throughout the school and beyond. Before long, concerned friends showed the circulating video to Mary and Ben, who were outraged. Herding up a posse, they sought out Sara and confronted her. They made clear how "not cool" it was to prey on their brother's innocence. They were still their

SPECIAL

brother's keeper, after all, and they were circling the wagons around him.

Mary and Ben found me afterwards and filled me in on it all. I knew Sara. She was a nice girl and a good student, who simply miscalculated the potential for harm with this new device...all for a laugh and some "likes." I have no doubt she grew from the incident for the commotion it generated. For his part, Daniel didn't get what the big deal was. He kind of liked the girls' rapt attention and was unable to grasp the social nuances involved.

Though figuring out the social etiquette of high school confounded Daniel at times, sports had no social nuances to navigate. During his high school years, Daniel became consumed by sports. He particularly liked football and baseball. Hoping to capitalize on this newfound passion, we gave him a miniature NFL football helmet display that had helmets for each of the thirty-two teams. Each Thursday he dutifully looked up the schedule of games for the week, arranging his picks across the display. Leading up to Thursday, he simply devoured the newspaper's sports page and sporting websites, citing injury reports, stats, anything he could find to substantiate his picks—all this from the boy who would be "lucky to read road signs." I'd say he definitely exceeded expectations.

However, as Daniel's love for sports blossomed, we saw a contrary trend begin to emerge. Daniel was more often than not rooting for rival Minnesotan teams, much to the chagrin of his family and friends devoted to the local sports scene. For football, his favorite team was the Green Bay Packers. While for baseball, he sided with any team currently playing the Minnesota Twins. It didn't matter what the team, they were his new favorite. We have often wondered aloud why Daniel

JOY CLINE

so vehemently roots against Minnesota, when his family flies the local sports flags. Perhaps it's a rebellious streak in him that exerts its independence in a safe manner. Or maybe the act of defying the local teams allows Daniel to exact a sense of control in a world where so many choices are yet made for him. Whatever the case, he bled green and gold.

Many people are surprised to hear this about Daniel. He can be a chameleon with his allegiances, seemingly shifting with his audience and their preferences. A classmate donning a Minnesota jersey might predict a dominant Vikings victory, to which Daniel would quickly chirp. "I agree with you," though a perusal of his picks for the week would say otherwise. A family friend, knowing Daniel is going to a Twins game, might ask him about his favorite Twins player. "Joe Mauer," would be his parroted response. But at the game itself, Daniel would glee in every strikeout Joe Mauer notched. His hair stylist might wonder if he's excited to watch the Viking's big game that Sunday, to which Daniel would wildly nod his assent while rattling off all the injuries the team must overcome.

That's the people pleaser in him, and it especially comes out with those he doesn't know well or with those he seeks to be aligned. But with those who know him well or who share his allegiances, he is unabashed in his teams of choice. And he can be pretty impassioned about it.

Daniel's best buddy during his high school years was Jake. Theirs was a friendship that burgeoned over their mutual love of sports. They talked endlessly each night, promptly at 7:00, about upcoming games. They simulated games of Madden football on their PlayStation consoles. They attended games together. But there was a major difference between the two of them...Daniel was a Green Bay Packers fan, while Jake liked the Minnesota Vikings. A great and vast divide. They were mostly able to coexist, friendship intact, throughout the NFL season, content to agree to disagree agreeably. Of course, two weeks a season—Packers/Vikings weeks—the gloves came off...literally.

One fall day of subbing I got a call from the assistant principal, asking me to drop by his office when I got a chance. My interest piqued, it didn't take long for me to be at his door.

"Hey, Joy," began Mr. Miller, "I just wanted to let you know that Daniel and Jake Sylvers got in a scuffle today in the hallway. They were arguing over the Packers and Vikings, and Daniel began shoving Jake around." While there was a serious tone to his voice, a smirk betrayed his words. "Now I've already talked to the boys and sent them back to class. Daniel was pretty remorseful, but I just wanted to let you know what had happened."

I thanked him for letting me know, leaving his office uncertain of the severity of the incident for the mixed message I received. Daniel had never been aggressive, and I didn't want him to begin now, just as he was gaining strength and stature. Besides, this was Jake, his best buddy, we were talking about! Geoff and I took it very seriously, shocked that a football game could evoke such intensity of emotions in him to become physically aggressive. After talking it through with Daniel, we took cues from his elementary days and created a social story for him to employ whenever emotions got the best of him in the sports realm. It's safe to say he's had a lot of practice over the years. As the game clock ticks down on a painful loss, Daniel is quick to offer his hand in congratulations and

JOY CLINE

say, "Good game," even when—hardest of all—it's a Viking's victory.

Daniel began his freshman year mostly contained in his DCD classroom. His one elective class was a class called Let's Eat! It cannot be denied—Daniel loves food, making it a seemingly good fit. But Daniel's true passion was music. By the time second trimester rolled around, his teachers had heard his heartbeat and enrolled him in Men's Choir. Men's Choir was a collection of guys, freshmen to seniors, who loved to sing but also have fun. Daniel fit right in. And with Mr. Uttecht at the helm, it was a safe place for him to pursue both. Mr. Uttecht further bequeathed himself to Daniel with his allegiance to the Green Bay Packers.

As in middle school, choir became Daniel's favorite hour of the day, as he shook the confines of the DCD classroom for the musical wing at FHS. The Cline name was revered in those halls, in large part due to the musical successes of Mary and Ben, who were both all-staters and members of the Minnesota Youth Jazz Band. But Daniel held his own in those halls. He would go on to spend all his remaining days at FHS with Men's Choir somewhere in it. And while he perhaps didn't have the musical prodigiousness of his siblings, his ever-present smile and friendliness endeared him to other students.

For our part, we marveled at our son up on the stage. In high school, the musical bar was set even higher in its expectations and difficulty. And while we grew used to Cline children occupying the musical spotlight and commanding its applause, Daniel's modest accomplishments were equally satisfying for the arduous journey they reflected. He still took his cues from the boys around him in the choreographed numbers, but his voice began to hit its mark, even as it deepened.

Daniel also began to hit his mark athletically. To be sure, he was still competing in bowling for the Farmington Tiger Paws in Special Olympics where stirring a competitive fire within him remained elusive. But within this season, a new door opened for him to compete.

Daniel's love of baseball was evident from an early age, despite the grimace he sported from his first outing as a catcher. Perhaps he took cues from Geoff's love of the game and his commitment to play ball with the boys, no matter how tired

he was from work. Whatever the case, Daniel developed an understanding of the game that defied his disability, as well as a contentment to follow Twins radio broadcasts through to the very last pitch. On a teacher's recommendation, we seized on this spark and had him try out for the Blazing Cats' softball team.

The Blazing Cats are a high school adaptive sports team consisting of athletes from Burnsville, Farmington, and Lakeville that participate in soccer, floor hockey, and softball. They compete

JOY CLINE

state wide in the Minnesota State High School League against other teams with cognitive impairments.

Daniel joined the squad as a lefty with great hand/eye coordination—a winning combination. And so while he was not a juggernaut at fielding or in firing in a throw, he did make a consistent, reliable presence behind the plate as a catcher. Offensively, his was a dependable bat in the lineup. He made the varsity as a sophomore and started every game.

Daniel picked up on the competitive zeal of his teammates and quickly learned this was not a team content to merely exude good sportsmanship. There was no letting others go first or cow towing to kindnesses. They wanted to win...badly, and they happened to do so a lot. Daniel joined a veteran squad that first year, earning a trip to the state tourney where they placed third. With success, notoriety around the school increased. Daniel and his Farmington Blazing Cats teammates were invited as guests on the set of the school's weekly television broadcast, *The Charlie Wierke Show.* While Daniel said little in the interview, content to allow his teammates command the microphone as he mostly nodded in assent, he was enamored at being on camera. He was and is to this day, a devoted follower of Farmington's weekly television spot on YouTube. Having Charlie, a senior and fellow Packer buddy, as the one to interview him and acknowledge the team's accomplishments only sealed the deal. He was hooked.

Bolstered by the experience, Daniel would go on to compete for the Blazing Cats' floor hockey and soccer teams as well. This adapted league was definitely a step up from our Special Olympics experiences. There was an intensity to the games that took me by surprise. Adaptive sports shrink the field of play to the confines of an indoor gym space. Bodies fly around everywhere in the name of competition...never mind

SPECIAL

that these are disabled athletes. Their talents defy that label. In fact, teammate Steven Friday celebrated every Blazing Cats' victory with a signature backflip. These were athletes with no asterisk behind their names.

Most games, Geoff and I were able to simply enjoy the talent on display as the Blazing Cats coasted to commanding leads. Playoff and state tournament games, however, were another matter. The competition intensified, and the stakes heightened. That intensity was palatable to us as spectators. We gasped. We cheered. We fumed...all in the name of a friendly competition.

Daniel's coaches, Dave Diehl and Shawn Tatge, exacted a fire out of him that we were never able to ignite, even with dangling cable television over him. To see my son enter the fray and tussle with the opponent for position or possession was something we never thought possible, docile boy that he was.

Most memorable of his Blazing Cats' stints was their run to the state softball championship his junior year. Daniel was playing catcher and hitting near the top of the order. Now in their second season together, he and pitcher Brenden Wong had developed a chemistry that was pretty much automatic. Brenden pitched strikes, and Daniel caught them and lobbed them back in sync. They were a thing of beauty to behold for the lack of drama they generated. Yet despite this connection, the Cats found themselves in a tight battle with the Osseo Orioles in the semifinals. Daniel had the hot bat that game, connecting for several key hits at critical junctures. Still, the game came down to the final inning with the Cats clinging to a slim one-run lead with an opponent on third. The Oriole batter ripped a ball just past the infield where Friday snagged it and rifled it into Daniel at home plate to prevent the player at third from scoring. Daniel fielded the throw and applied a nifty game-saving tag to squash the threat and assure the Blazing Cats a spot in the championship game. In Blazing Cats' lore, it became known simply as "The Tag," and it found its way captured for posterity in the pages of the *Minneapolis Star Tribune* the next morning.

The Blazing Cats would go on to win the championship game the next day in much less dramatic fashion. And for his efforts, Daniel earned a spot on the all-tournament team. All told, the Blazing Cats would amass two state championships, two runner-up trophies, a third and a fifth place finish during Daniel's tenure. While not attaining dynasty status, they did have a pretty good run. Greater still, we were left to relish the huge growth, particularly in Daniel's intensity to compete, reflected in that run. Between Men's Choir and the Blazing Cats, Daniel was truly hitting his stride at FHS, both literally and figuratively. He fairly raced through his days, a chorus of

SPECIAL

"Hi Daniel's" following him. There was an unabated joy written across his face in the form of his ever-present smile. In fact, upon seeing Daniel dash past the office one day, the school attendance secretary turned to me and asked, "Is he *always* this happy?"

After a moment's thought, I nodded, "Yea, pretty much."

Before we knew it, spring was upon us...the last spring of high school. While most seniors incessantly count the days to graduation, their counts posted on whiteboards scattered about the school, Daniel did not want to see his high school days come to an end. He regularly deflected any talk of the ceremony that would mark the end of all he loved and propel him into a future that was just as uncertain. Planning for his grad party was an admission of the impending end, and he avoided it at all costs. But soon the unavoidable was upon us, and we were staring into another season of lasts...the last choir concert, the last ball game, the last state tourney. It was in that flurry of activity that we experienced, perhaps, the most unlikeliest of blessings.

Prom was rapidly approaching, and to be in the schools was not to miss it. Couples were pairing up, girls were poring over the internet in search of the perfect dress, and extravagant dinner plans were being finalized. Also being finalized was the royalty court for prom, voted on by the senior class during their Tiger Time. I was subbing in the EBD wing of the school when the announcement of finalists was made. Attending to the students in front of me, I only managed bits and pieces of the announcement. Besides, beyond offering congratulations to the students selected, what importance did the principal's words hold for me?

JOY CLINE

But that is where I underestimated the Unsinkable Daniel Cline. Into my classroom walked one of my fellow teachers, offering her congratulations. I looked back at her blankly.

"Daniel!" She exclaimed. "He was just chosen for prom court!"

I was stunned. This was a first for the Cline family, and I hardly knew how to respond. It threw me, but in a good way.

Not long afterwards, one of Daniel's teachers brought him up to see me and share in the joy of the moment. Still bursting from the unexpected news, I fairly bowled Daniel over in a big embrace. Just as unexpectedly though, he pulled back, rebuffing me. His response surprised me. Daniel nearly always welcomed my hugs. Why not now? And why not especially in this time of great celebration? I have learned that for all of Daniel's autistic penchants for routine and predictability, he can still throw me for a loop sometimes. This was one of those moments.

Prom was just a week away, thrusting us into a flurry of preparations. Daniel had never expressed an interest in prom, and Geoff and I were certainly not ones to push it. I think in our minds it was our way of shielding him from the pain of rejection, hurt, or humiliation in the cruel world of dating. Yet Daniel craved inclusion, even if he wasn't able to find his voice to articulate it. In being selected to the prom court, Daniel had executed the perfect end-around. He was going to be in prom's grand march and coronation, in spite of his parents' sheltering ways!

That weekend, Daniel and I went looking for a suit at JCPenneys. I figured he needed to look the part amongst all the prom-goers. But while I could size him up for a suit that made him fit in, there was no certainty he would ever acquiesce to actually wearing it. His tactile sensitivities still set the tone for his wardrobe, and I was sure he would fight the constriction of the suit. He was always quick to rip off any tie he had been roped into. We ended up buying him a black suit with an aqua shirt and matching tie. He looked incredibly handsome.

On the Wednesday before prom, I was subbing for AP Psychology and had a senior Tiger Time class. The senior class was to vote for the prom king and queen through a voting link on their iPads. There was a buzz in the air that day, a tangible excitement rippling through each of my classes. It gave me pause to hope.

We found that Daniel had been paired with Anna Korbein for the coronation ceremony. Anna was the perfect companion for him on the red carpet. She had spent years volunteering in his classroom and would go on to a future as a special education teacher. She had an established connection with Daniel, and she made him feel comfortable and calm in the enormity of the day...or at least as comfortable as could be expected in a suit. While not eschewing the suit altogether, I think Daniel figured it was a necessary evil that enabled him to be one of the crowd. We kept the top button of his shirt undone and loosened his tie a bit, and he was ready for his grand entrance.

Our whole family was squished together in the gym's stands with longtime friends alongside for support. The master of ceremonies for the coronation was Mr. Gottwig, the legendary

JOY CLINE

band director. At the time, I thought how fitting it was to have Mr. Gottwig introducing Daniel and Anna for the prominent role he had played in Mary and Ben's high school experience. He always had a soft spot for Daniel as the only Cline *not* in band. He announced Daniel and Anna, and the spotlight followed them. They were a striking pair. Reminded repeatedly to walk slowly and hold out his arm just so for Anna, Daniel was the perfect gentleman. He escorted her to the runway's end where they parted for their places—Anna to her line of girls on the right and Daniel to his guys on the left.

The boys joining Daniel on the prom court were an impressive collection in their own right. One was headed to Princeton on a full ride scholarship, another was the leader of the choir who always made time for Daniel, while yet another was a football star who would become a fellow classmate down the road. Before each of the candidates was a bag with a gift-wrapped rose that would reveal their fate—white for courtly status and red for royalty. When instructed to open their roses, Daniel—in fitting Daniel form—held back from unwrapping his own flower, content to allow the drama to unfold through the other boys' unwrappings. When he could delay no longer, he gingerly picked away at his own paper until a red rose emerged.

Simultaneously, the girls were opening their own roses. As fate would have it, the red one landed in the hands of Katie Aaron. If Anna had been the perfect companion for the runway, Katie was even more perfect alongside Daniel as his queen. Katie had a genuineness about her. She was a kind soul who had given up her own senior Tiger Time to hang out in Daniel's classroom playing UNO, chatting away, and generally being a good friend to some students who could use one. Daniel certainly needed a good friend beside him for the enormity of the moment. He was never one to clamber to the spotlight. And while Daniel is a people person, there were just so many people and so many pictures. Knowing Daniel as she did, Katie stepped back to allow Daniel to bask in the moment, but stepped in when his focus faltered. She let him have his voice, but spoke for him when words failed him. Everyone should have a Katie alongside them for the big moments of life.

Eventually, the well wishers dwindled, and our fairytale was seemingly ending. We went to collect Daniel. But before we were able to leave, two of Daniel's special education teachers, who conveniently also doubled as prom committee leads, rushed over to catch us and propose an offer we couldn't refuse.

"Would Daniel like to go to prom tonight?" asked Mrs. Revels. "Jenni and I will be there, and we'll keep an eye out for him."

"But he doesn't have a ticket," I ventured.

To which they merely waved the thought aside. "He belongs."

Belonging, I thought, isn't that what he's always wanted—to belong? I turned to Daniel, "What do you think? Do you want to go to prom?" Before I had even finished, he was nodding his head in wild assent. It was settled.

JOY CLINE

Not having lavish dinner plans, we headed home to hot dogs, while Mary and Ben drove back to college and their impending semester finals. For all the hoopla of his crowning, Daniel remained pretty much unfazed. He got home, ripped off his jacket and tie, turned on the Twins, and resumed calling pitch counts...albeit with a crown on his head.

When it came time to take off for the dance, Geoff retied Daniel's tie, and we loaded into the minivan. "So where are we headed?" He asked.

I looked at Geoff with uncertainty, realizing I had missed out on a rather important detail. "I know it's near the Mall of America."

Geoff pulled up iMaps on his phone. "There's the new Radisson hotel."

Trying desperately to recall the prom details from the past week's school announcements, I said, "Yea, that sounds about right." And off we went.

When we got to the hotel, there was little room for parking, so Geoff dropped Daniel and me off at the front door and went to find some place to park. On a quick survey of the lobby, I was surprised to not see any other students arriving for the evening. The hotel was actually called the Radisson Blu, and it had only been open about a year. The place sparkled, and I thought what a stylish venue this was for a prom. Unsure of the location in the hotel for the evening's festivities, Daniel and I sought help from the hotel's concierge.

"Could you help us find where Farmington's prom is taking place?" I asked the woman behind the desk. I'm sure we were quite the sight...Daniel all dressed up, crown still intact,

SPECIAL

and me not so much. There was a definite air of superiority emanating from her.

"Not here," was her clipped response.

"Are there any other Radisson hotels nearby?"

"Not that I'm aware of." And I knew that was the end of our conversation.

Greater still, I realized I now had no idea where prom was actually being held. Geoff pulled up and we jumped into the van, pondering our next move. We called a friend whose son was also attending prom that night. He was able to point us to the hotel being located on American Boulevard. That was a start. Pulling up iMaps again, we found there were exactly eleven hotels matching that criteria. Off we went. We started at the far western edge of the strip and worked our way eastward. We stopped at each hotel, looking for any activity that might mark it as the location for prom. With each quiet facade, we began to lose hope. Yet we dutifully checked off each hotel and moved on to the next. After about the fourth hotel, our friend called us back. He had checked in with his son, who was able to pinpoint the exact location.

As we approached the hotel, the welcome activity of students arriving in limousines and party buses assured us that we had, at last, hit our mark. We found Mrs. Revels and Ms. Guite, who whisked Daniel away to the evening fun, while Geoff and I settled into some chairs in the lobby to await Daniel's return. And though Geoff and I never actually set foot in prom's reverie, it seems it was worth the pursuit. Of course, in Daniel's own words, it was "good." It would be in the days that followed that we would get a clearer picture of the life-giving evening it had been for him. It came in pictures posted on Facebook. It

came in the gift of a strip of pictures from a photo booth. And it came from the stories from teachers and students alike that filled in the gaps and reassured us that our son had had the time of his life being king for a day. Perhaps he even had too great of a time being king. For when Monday rolled around and it was time for school, Daniel came down for breakfast with the crown still perched atop his head.

"Daniel, why are you still wearing your crown?"

"I want to wear it to school today."

I hadn't considered this, and I cringed at the thought of him wearing the crown to school for the ridicule it would certainly invite. But Daniel seemed determined. And heck, when will you ever get the chance to be king again in life? Jake later posted a picture from the day of the two best friends smiling widely. Despite the tussle from a few years earlier, the two remained inseparable. Beyond Jake, it seems the crown was an endearing artifact. In fact, Daniel was treated to hero status amongst his special education peers for his brush with royalty, and he seemed to wear the crown well. Yet when Tuesday dawned, he was able to finally relinquish it to the shelf.

That chapter behind us, graduation was now looming large on the calendar, and Daniel could no longer avoid the inevitable. On June 6th, the Cline family was in force, seated on the football stadium's field for the commencement activities of Farmington's Class of 2014. Incidentally, Daniel's was the first class to hold their graduation ceremony in the new school's

SPECIAL

stadium, the result of four years of inopportune rain. It was a beautiful evening. As the students prepared to receive their diplomas, Principal Jason Berg asked the audience to hold its applause until all students had received their diplomas. I have always felt sorry for the students whose last names begin with an A, whose celebration is curtailed by the inhibitions of propriety. Fortunately for Daniel, by the time they got to the C's, protocol had been abandoned. As Daniel strode across the stage to collect his certificate of achievement, his classmates erupted in a sustained cheer, the loudest of the evening so far. But then, who am I to judge? I'm the mom.

As inauspicious as his start and through the leveling of middle school, could we have ever imagined the ending of these days in the Farmington schools? To witness his peers, those same peers from elementary and middle school, come full circle to actually elevating Daniel by their votes and applause. It was a beautiful transformation, not lost on me. For as a parent of a special needs child, I had been conditioned not to hold too high of expectations for my child, the result of countless IEP meetings dousing my hopes and dreams. Yet Daniel exceeded those expectations. God gave me a front row seat to my son's resilience through the challenging seasons so I could appreciate all the more profoundly the heights. And to think that back in my day, Daniel would have spent his education shuttered away. What an incredible loss…on all accounts!

JOY CLINE

12

EMBEDDED SECURITIES

For all the impending dread of his final days at Farmington High School, Daniel quickly discovered that life after graduation wasn't so bad after all. Of course, there were the endless grad parties that nearly rolled right into the new school term and that added several unwanted pounds. There was also summer, which in its activity easily relinquished the past school year into the rearview mirror. And perhaps easiest of all was the understanding that his school days weren't exactly over, they were just different now.

In the fall, Daniel began a three-year stint at the TESA (Transitional Ed Service Alternative) Program at Dakota County Technical College in nearby Rosemount. TESA is a post-secondary program servicing recent special education graduates from neighboring communities. It offers students the chance to grow their independent living and employment skills. What it didn't offer so much were academic pursuits, extracurricular activities, or inclusive opportunities—some of Daniel's favorite parts of high school.

But much like high school, Daniel still boarded a Farmington bus each morning that took him to DCTC and dropped him off at our driveway in the afternoon. In fact, many of the same bus drivers who had been driving Daniel for years also made the Rosemount run and were a huge part of making the transition to TESA such a seamless one. The history they shared made for great banter and laughter on the monotonous trips to and

JOY CLINE

from school. Much to Daniel's delight, these same bus drivers held daily "races" as to which Farmington bus would get to town first. Daniel never tired of this game with all the variables in play in a fifteen-minute drive: from stoplights to inopportune trains and traffic delays.

Before long, Daniel had fully settled into his post high school days. Though not as busy as he had been, he found a comfort in home life. And we certainly made it comfortable for him by holding him to few expectations. Mary and Ben were both away at college at the time, allowing Daniel the full run of the house…his computer, his television, his PlayStation. Of course, Geoff and I kept him well fed and clothed, and were his ever-present companions. What more could he want? It was a sweet season for him. It was also a season where we saw some of Daniel's embedded securities become more pronounced.

Daniel has always derived great security from certain things: predictable routines, his dog, and even his stuffed animals. Daniel had lots of stuffed animals, each chosen for the season of life he was currently in. His favorites, hands down though, were Georgie the green gorilla and Barney the dinosaur— or Binks, as we called him. Funny thing about Georgie and Binks…they weren't Daniel's to begin with. He inherited them from his siblings. Ben was given Georgie from some friends, and Mary had Binks, as she had been an avid *Barney the Dinosaur* fan from the heyday of his run on PBS. But with time and maturity, both stuffed animals eventually languished from neglect at Ben and Mary's hands, while Daniel kind of took a liking to them. Georgie reminded him of one of his favorite book characters, Curious George, and Daniel still had no inhibitions about watching *Barney the Dinosaur* on TV. He latched onto both, and they became officially his.

SPECIAL

But to Daniel, they were so much more than carefully crafted bags of stuffing. They became his companions and comfort, each with his own unique personality. Binks was the tried and true loyal friend, who always tried to do what was right. He was kind to a fault and played by the rules. George Man? Not so much. Georgie was the emboldened one, ever finding himself in the thick of every situation. A friend to the devious, he pushed the limits and pressed boundaries, often with a sly giggle.

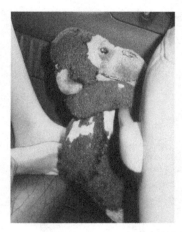

Both became an extension of Daniel in so many ways. Foremost, of course, was by their very presence. Daniel rarely went to bed without the two of them at his side, not even for sleepovers. His friends got used to them being unabashedly in tow. When we got in the car, so did Georgie and Binks, each latched in behind the two front seats with George Man assuming the driver's position. The two joined us for all our family trips. And while Binks was largely welcomed, Georgie quickly soured on us. In fact, George Man chose marathon cross-country road trips for some of his most fiendish schemes. Subsequently, if not for Daniel's ardent pleas, he would have been banished from the car with an unceremonious fling at several junctures of our trips. Yet they both endured and even came along with us for boat rides at the cabin, Georgie joining Daniel at the captain's wheel. Riders beware when George Man was at the helm! The pontoon sped and slowed and swerved and skirted the shoreline. Gramps never much liked "the monkey!"

JOY CLINE

As time went on, we saw a shift from the two serving as mere companions to becoming Daniel's crutches for the challenging situations of life. Senior pictures with their endless positionings and cued smiles with eyes open, heightened his anxieties. George Man came along for the shoot and, with his comic relief, eased the stress. Hikes in Banff that exacted strength, endurance, and fearlessness on queasy heights were made more manageable with "the guys" tucked away in Daniel's and Geoff's backpacks, heads popped out for a view. And we especially found ways to include Georgie and Binks as constants for Daniel that somehow steadied him for the change that was before him in the big transitions of life.

Daniel became so attached to his stuffed animals that he even began to project himself through them. When he didn't know what to say to engage conversation, Georgie and Binks gave him the words. Each had a distinct voice of their own, as Daniel altered his own to give them one. He always spoke more freely under their personas. But beyond giving him a voice, they became an extension of his very personality. Daniel is definitely more like Binks—the kind, yielding, rule follower.

SPECIAL

But there is a part of him that longs to be Georgie, the one who stirs the pot and garnishes the laughs.

As much as Georgie and Binks had become an extension of Daniel's life, we found they had also become an extension of our entire family as well. When Mary and Ben went off to Mexico for a mission's trip, Ben brought back a green sombrero for Georgie that fit him perfectly. And when Ben and Allison were married, Daniel had Georgie alongside him for his groom's dinner toast. George Man looked the part, trading his sombrero for a top hat to welcome Allison into the family.

Nowadays, the two bear that look that ensures they are well loved. Georgie has several large patches of green fur missing from his belly and a nose nearly rubbed bare, while Binks is missing an eye and has had the stuffing shoved back in and sewn up tightly with stitchings upon stitchings. From time to time they are tossed in the wash to be freshened up a bit, always with the hope they will emerge all in one piece to assist Daniel through that next big step of life.

If Georgie and Binks were the stuffed companions from which Daniel derived comfort, our family dogs became the living equivalent for him. Just before Daniel started his educational journey, we got our first dog, a Border Collie we named Puck because with his black and white coloring he looked like a hockey puck on ice. Puck was everything a Border Collie should be: smart, energetic, and a herder. If we were to be honest, he probably had a little too much under the hood, so to speak, to be a great family dog…especially for such a young family as ours was at the time. Puck instinctively herded the kids around, as was his nature. He held them in check whenever things got a little too loud or a little too wild for his liking. He especially took his cue at bedtime. Typically we all read together before bed, capping off the evening ritual with a family prayer. As soon as Puck heard "Amen," he knew the chase was on! Up the steps ran all three Cline children with Puck at their heels, barking and containing them until they reached the second flight of stairs where their bedrooms were located and where he  wasn't allowed to go. Frustrated, he often slammed the kitchen door closed with his muzzle, sometimes taking a bite at it for good measure. Our kitchen door definitely became a conversation starter over the years!

 For his part, Puck mostly endured the tormenting of the kids…the clothes they would dress him in, the balls they would hide from him, and the endless games of hide and seek they would play with him. As the youngest, Daniel was probably chief amongst his tormentors. Yet Daniel loved Puck and loved the idea of having a dog. Puck became Daniel's loyal fishing partner up at the cabin, herding the

SPECIAL

bobber as it was reeled in, hoping there was a fish on the end of the line. He even fell in a time or two, so intense his focus. As the kids grew up and Puck aged as well, we all kind of grew into one another better in all the mellowing.

For our second Border Collie, we consciously chose one with a little less moxie—the runt of the litter. We named her Lizzy; and while she still bore the characteristic Border Collie tendencies, she definitely was a step down from Puck and altogether sweet in her temperament. The kids were all in high school when we brought Lizzy home at a mere seven weeks old. Despite their promises otherwise, we quickly discovered that their busy high school schedules meant I would be her main caregiver.

Daniel particularly latched on to Lizzy. Here was a dog that he actually outsized and over which he could actually exact some measure of control. As the youngest, I think that was kind of refreshing for him. And with Mary and Ben heading off for college the next couple years after her arrival to the family, Lizzy became almost like a surrogate sibling to Daniel in their absence. He was Lizzy's designated ball retriever and thrower, and she was a dog that required lots of balls thrown…at least eighty a day, to be exact. Daniel was the one, besieged by her begging, who slipped her food from time to time. She was especially fond of popcorn. Whenever Daniel had to be away from home, his first thoughts were for his dog: "What's Lizzy doing?" "Has she had her walk yet?" "Did you remember her treats?" And to receive a birthday card from Daniel meant a picture of Lizzy prominently featured somewhere on it. She was a pet he could wrap his arms around, bury his face in her fur, and know

JOY CLINE

her love in return in the warm, sloppy licks from her sandpaper pink tongue. As one with autism and for whom conveying feelings and emotions is difficult, Lizzy somehow made it easy.

One Memorial Day, when Daniel was gearing up for his summer softball season, Geoff took him outside to practice batting. Daniel had a ball machine that would pop up balls for him to swing at when he activated it. As was often the case, Lizzy joined Geoff as the ball shagger, chasing down Daniel's hits. If we didn't let her join in the game, she would race from window to door and back again, barking incessantly in protest. It was easier to just let her join in the fun and run off some energy.

This particular day, I was inside cleaning up from lunch when I heard alarming shouts from outside. I rushed to the door to see Geoff bent over, crying in anguish, "No, no…oh please, God, no!" I knew something was incredibly wrong. I rushed out the door and around the house only to find Lizzy crumpled to the ground trembling, and Daniel beside her, bat still in his hand, wailing, "Help! Help! Help!" I scooped her into my arms, while Geoff got a cold, wet towel that we pressed against her forehead to stop the bleeding. Geoff and I jumped into the car and headed to the emergency vet clinic a twenty-minute drive away, leaving Daniel at home because his heart just might break from the weight of it all.

En route, Geoff gave me the story in bits and pieces as his grief would allow. Apparently, when Daniel tapped his ball machine, the ball popped up a little off kilter—enough so, that he hesitated just briefly before adjusting to make his swing. That brief adjustment was all the time Lizzy needed. In his hesitation, she lunged for the ball, instead of first waiting for him to hit it so she could give chase. Daniel's bat came down hard, landing near her eye and sending her sprawling. It all happened so very fast.

SPECIAL

As I held her in my arms—whimpering, trembling, and in obvious pain—I was certain she was slipping into shock. I figured she was bleeding internally in her skull. And in that belief, I was under the understanding I was holding my dog for the last time. We prayed over her, and Geoff called the vet as he drove so that they were ready for us when we arrived with a stretcher with which to whisk her away.

Left to await the vet's life-saving efforts, we were numb by how our day could change so dramatically. But we also both began shooting out texts to family and friends alike to just pray. And while some might say she is merely a dog, the situation held so much more in the complexity of it all. For in my mind, we were praying for Daniel just as much as for Lizzy, if not more so. The thought that his beloved dog might die at his hands, though an accident, would crush him, so great his love for her and so sensitive his spirit. The intersection of these two tore me apart in its possibility.

When the vet finally emerged after a couple of hours, we held our breath in anticipation of the news. But it was not the news we dreaded. Instead, buoyed by a community of prayers, the news was better than we ever could have imagined! The vet had managed to sedate her, address the damage, manage the pain, and set her on a course towards recovery. While she wasn't quite out of the woods just yet, he warned, he believed that if she survived the night, she just might make it through. We headed home hopeful and kept the phone next to our bed, hoping we didn't hear from him. Yet around 5:00 the next morning, the phone rang. It was the clinic, and we held our breaths a second time.

"We just wanted to let you know that Lizzy is doing as well as can be expected. You're free to come get her any time before 9:00, when we go off duty. We'll update you with her care plan then."

And with those words, we let out a deep sigh of relief. We knew Lizzy would live to see another day, and we couldn't wait to share the news with Daniel! All told, her recovery took a few weeks. Her pain meds kept her mostly sedentary or asleep during that time, but we had our dog—Daniel's buddy—back.

Her eye socket had been partially crushed, disfiguring her face slightly, and she would be forever inconvenienced by a persistent weepy right eye. But all that mattered little for the companionship her presence restored. It wasn't long before Daniel resumed throwing balls for her, but they never did play the batting game again. Those wounds would remain too fresh for memory.

For all of Daniel's embedded securities, his need for a predictable routine trumped all others—greater than Georgie and Binks, greater even than Puck and Lizzy. He took comfort in knowing what was ahead of him at any particular time on any particular day. Though not a list guy per se, you can bet he is ticking things off in his head. When he doesn't think anyone is listening, he will reel through his day. The schedule steadies him and gives him a sense of control. Knowing what is before him, he is better able to prepare himself.

Of course, life laughs at predictability. The reality is that there are always the unexpected, the wrenches that get thrown in our plans from which we need to adjust and adapt. As one with autism, one of Daniel's great challenges in life is to learn flexibility in the face of the unexpected. While we, as parents, try to provide him the structure of predictable routines that bring him the security he yearns for, we also know he needs opportunities of unpredictability to grow resilient and adapting.

SPECIAL

Yet exposing him to different experiences has often been met with resistance. Daniel's rigidity to a schedule keeps him from trying new things, content to remain unchallenged in the familiar rhythms. It is a never-ending balancing act of comfort and growth.

Fortunately, his time at school provided a classroom for both. School is, by nature, very schedule driven, and Daniel thrived under its predictability. He was especially attuned to what was supposed to happen next at any given stage of his day. Pity the teacher who tried to mix things up by changing the day around. Daniel was quick to point out any deviants from the schedule, whether intentional or unintentional. He was very time conscious and kept them all on their toes. That said, whenever testing for special education services rolled around, we learned to have the clock removed from the room so he could focus on the work at hand. The clock remained that constant reminder of all that he was missing back in the classroom, and Daniel hated missing out on any part of his day!

School had set the schedule for so much of his life that as we entered Daniel's last year of TESA and looked out onto an uncertain horizon void of school and its structure, we did so with trepidation. We knew we needed to get a plan in place for his future, but what would that plan be? We didn't know.

As the year came to an end and Daniel boarded the bus for his last ride home from DCTC, you can bet there was a race to Farmington on the way home. The bus stopped at our driveway, and the door swung open. Daniel's longtime bus driver and bus aide stepped off the bus with him to acknowledge the journey it had been—some 6,400 bus rides, by my count. The tears spilling out of his eyes, Mark the bus driver said, "I'm going to miss you, Daniel." And I knew he meant it.

13

THE THIRD OPTION

There were reminders everywhere that this was the last year of TESA and with it, the last year of Daniel's educational journey. From notices we received for housing and employment fairs to meetings scheduled for post-graduation planning to plans for graduation itself where Daniel would finally receive his high school diploma, we knew our days for figuring this whole life after school for Daniel had a defined number on it. For most of the seniors in Daniel's TESA program, there were two options after graduation: employment or a day program. With employment and transportation opportunities limited in Farmington, we sought a third option.

As an avid newspaper reader, an article from the *Minneapolis Star Tribune* caught my attention with its headline, "Minnesotans with Intellectual Disabilities Are New Kids on Campus."[7] The article told of a new program for young adults with intellectual disabilities at Bethel University in St. Paul, the very school where Ben was then a senior. Having that connection, I read on. Twelve students, aged 18 to 24, were settling in as the first cohort of the BUILD Program (Bethel University Inclusive Learning and Development). Bethel billed itself as Minnesota's first four-year accredited college to offer a two-year residential program for students with intellectual disabilities. I shared the article with Geoff.

---

[7] Burger, K. (2015, October 4). *Minnesotans with intellectual disabilities are New Kids on Campus.* Star Tribune. https://www.startribune.com/minnesotans-with-intellectual-disabilities-are-new-kids-on-campus/330411671

SPECIAL

I have always been a Bethel fan, knowing it to be a solid Christian university. I had a good friend with whom I had journeyed alongside through her Masters of Children's Ministry program at the seminary. I learned from her experience that Bethel was incredibly intentional about creating a space for community to form. Of course, Geoff and I believed in Bethel enough to rubber stamp Ben's decision to study there. We knew it to be a place where faith is not dictated, but able to become a student's own. Ben's faith strengthened under such nurturing conditions that welcomed challenge and exploration, while providing vast opportunities to connect spiritually with other students and staff.

And while Ben thrived at Bethel, much of that thriving had to do with the deep relationships he formed along the way. Some of the first friends were the guys on his dorm floor. Soon others joined the circle from assorted associations. They were a posse, and they were tight. There were weekend adventures around the Twin Cities, challenging conversations over coffee, and road trips together through snow storms. They set roots for a lifetime from a shared beginning at Bethel where relationships were steeped in their common bond as Jesus followers. Ben not only found lifelong friends at college, but also a lifelong mate. Allison was a Bethel grad as well. And although they didn't start dating until after their college days were over, such was the fabric of Bethel's community that they were well aware of one another.

From time to time we played host to Ben's posse. It might be having a group of them for dinner en route to a Bethel hockey game, throwing a view party for team USA in the 2014 World Cup, or even pulling out some inflatable mattresses for an overnighter for a local band performance. It was always an engaging and lively time as we got to better know Ben's friends of significance.

JOY CLINE

One spring night, not long before his college graduation, Ben asked if he could bring a group home for dinner and a bonfire. Of course we said yes. Conversation around the table was bent towards future plans, as they were looking ahead to the impending end of their Bethel days. Before long, they got up from the table to venture outside for a perfect night around the fire pit. But before leaving, one of the guys turned back, seemingly on a whim, and asked,"Would you like to come with us, Daniel?"

I braced myself for Daniel to turn them down, such was his dogged allegiance to his nightly routines. Rarely is the allure attractive enough to wrest him from his plans. On top of it all, the Twins were playing that night on television...the final nail in the coffin, in my mind. But then Daniel did something totally unexpected.

"Yes," he said.

And with that "yes," he fell in line behind them and headed out to the fire. Throughout the evening, I slipped out to see if they needed anything, though I was really gauging whether Daniel was wearing out his welcome. What I saw, instead, was Ben and his friends making him feel as one of them. They actively drew him into conversations and shared insider jokes with him. He ate it up. As it became dark, I kept waiting for him to retreat to the house for a Twins score update, but he didn't. Seeing him laughing and so engaged with the group, my mind went to Bethel's BUILD Program, and I thought, "This is what life at Bethel could look like for Daniel." And I began to ask, "What if...?"

For his part, Daniel was happy as could be in the status quo. He was comfortable at home with its routines, familiarity, relative comfort, and low expectations. But Geoff and I caught

SPECIAL

a vision that night in the abundant interactions that life could be so much more for Daniel.

That thought fresh on my mind, we were at Bethel a lot that spring for all those events marking the end of Ben's time there. Though now, I looked at Bethel through the fresh eyes of possibility. One of those events was a luncheon for Ben, honoring him with the Elizabeth A. Hossler Outstanding Psychology Student award as the top psychology student graduating from the program.

In the course of the luncheon, we were able to meet all of Ben's psychology professors and advisors who had been such an integral part of his time at Bethel. One conversation, in particular, stuck with me. In talking with Ben's advisor during his tenure at Bethel, I happened to convey that Ben had a special needs brother for whom we were looking into the BUILD Program. She countered that she, too, had a special needs brother back in Montana. Such an advocate she was for him that she took up the charge at Bethel as well, serving on BUILD's planning board. That was all the opening I needed. I peppered her with questions about the program, trying to—in effect—gauge whether Daniel might be a good fit. Finally, we got down to the hard questions.

"Ben got scholarships, grants, and loans to help defray the cost of Bethel. How do students in the BUILD Program pay for college?"

She hemmed and hawed, and really didn't have an answer for me on that one. And in her silence, it was as if a pin was taken to all the hopes that had begun to mount for this possibility. I was deflated. At a total cost of just over $45,000 a year at the time, it outpaced our ability to finance such an opportunity. Heck, two years of Bethel would be in the range of our house

JOY CLINE

mortgage! As much as I longed for this for Daniel, the dream of Bethel, in my mind, was dead.

Still, when asked by Daniel's case manager, Callan Billings, at our annual renewal of services in the fall what our dreams for him were, we didn't hesitate. "Bethel," Geoff and I said in unison, hoping she could somehow find a way. And while at the time it was *our* dream, I'm pretty sure it wasn't Daniel's. Still in his days at TESA, he couldn't see beyond the present. And from where he stood, life seemed pretty good.

Callan wrote it down in her notes, and we thought that was the end of it. But about a month later, she forwarded us a notification that the BUILD Program met the requirements for our county's consideration as a viable transition option. What that exactly meant, we weren't certain; and Callan wasn't quite sure either. But there was enough hope in its wording that there just might be some help funding Bethel after all. Suddenly, the unsettled nature of Daniel's future had a potentially viable third option. Game on!

Seizing on that sliver of hope, we went online to the BUILD Program's website and scheduled a campus tour. By now, BUILD's Cohort Two had made its appearance on campus, though Daniel's tour would be led by a veteran from Cohort One, Maggie Erickson. When Maggie first introduced herself to us in the Admissions Office, I was struck by her poise and confidence. Here was a young Down syndrome woman who was comfortable in her own skin. She asked Daniel about his background and interests, taking special note for opportunities later in the tour to seize on these, and off we went for our tour. Having Ben as a recent graduate, we were familiar with Bethel's campus. The tour was all for Daniel's benefit: could he see himself at Bethel apart from Ben's overseeing influence?

SPECIAL

Maggie certainly did her part to make it easy! Her introductions to various locations on campus came sprinkled with interactions with those in the halls. Beyond mere greetings, these were real conversations that spoke of depth and relationship. It was impossible not to see that Maggie was a rock star on campus. Maggie's connections with students and staff alike tugged at a deep need within Daniel...the need for meaningful interactions. Bethel, it seemed, offered plenty of those! At the end of the visit, Daniel had shifted ever-so-slightly to entertaining the thought of a future at Bethel.

Always the opportunists, Geoff and I pounced on the feel good experience as an opening for Daniel. He willingly applied to Bethel with the understanding that he might not be accepted. In fact, I think he kind of banked on that in his compliance. But it was also in this discussion of attending Bethel that Geoff and I did something we had never done before for such a significant decision in Daniel's life...we uttered the words, "It's completely your decision." Daniel took those words to heart with vigor, inserting them whenever the topic of his pursuit of Bethel came up in conversations. In fact, those words got thrown back in our faces with such vehemence and frequency, we realized the mountain of resistance that was forming and began to regret ever giving Daniel such total control over his future.

The send button hit on the application to the BUILD Program, we waited. As we waited, we left Daniel's future at the Lord's feet. Leaning on Jesus' promise to His disciples from Matthew 18:19-20 that His presence is there in numbers, we assembled the support of others' prayers to topple what, in our minds, were such overwhelming odds.[8] We reached out to our family. We reached out to our small group. We reached out to our

---

[8] *Bible gateway passage: Matthew 18:19-20 - new international version.* Bible Gateway. (n.d.-i). https://www.biblegateway.com/passage/?search=Matthew+ 18%3A19-20&version=NIV

JOY CLINE

friends. Our requests were much the same to all. We needed God's help in three ways: that Daniel might be accepted into the BUILD Program, that he might actually be willing to attend, and that the Lord might provide the financial means to cover the cost. Those were three big prayers, and we felt a bit exposed in our faith in sharing them. Yet as we faithfully prayed for what became our Big Three, we ultimately desired God's overarching will to be done. We knew better than to reduce Him to genie status. His sovereign vantage ensured Daniel's best future—Bethel or not. We left it to His better plans.

Our emotions went up and down during the wait. Sometimes we had faith for Bethel and allowed ourselves to dream how it might change our lives. While at other times, the silence overpowered us with doubt. It was a couple of months into that wait that we received an email that sent us soaring: Daniel had been selected for an interview with the BUILD Program! We chose a date in December, and Geoff and I cleared our schedules. We also had our prayer warriors cover us in prayer for that interview. We knew if our Big Three were in alignment with God's higher will, all hinged on this first step.

The morning of the interview, Geoff and I actively sought to level down the tension with lightheartedness. Daniel has always been at his best when he is simply being Daniel—too many directives and too much advice stymies him. Apart from helping him choose an outfit for the interview, Geoff and I were pretty hands off, not wanting to raise his stress level. When we entered the Admissions Office, Kay made sure we were welcomed and cared for as we awaited our interview. Before long, we were greeted warmly by two women: Dawn Allen, the director of the BUILD Program, and Janelle Kelly, the assistant director. Though we had met them before as part of Daniel's tour, we took an immediate liking to them, and Daniel did as well! They both had a twinkle to their eye and genuinely

SPECIAL

pursued getting to know Daniel better. They were also quick to laugh, putting Daniel at ease. When they spoke, they mostly directed the conversation towards him, and we kind of liked that. He was feeling his kingly vibes all over again!

We began the interview all together, as Dawn and Janelle dug a little deeper into our family story with its hopes and dreams for Daniel. We were able to counter with a few of our own pressing questions about the program. We appreciated their frank, honest answers when we leveled our hard questions over financing. We felt they weren't holding back any punches; and in that, they earned our trust. By the time Geoff and I were ushered from the room so that Daniel could be further interviewed and tested, we were sold on the BUILD Program and hoped Daniel was as well.

Geoff and I settled into some chairs just outside the interview room to unpack all we had just heard and experienced. From our vantage point, we could see into the interview room through a set of windows. Daniel seemed comfortable and engaged. On our way to Bethel that morning, he had continued to reiterate to Geoff and me that the decision of going to Bethel was his. But somehow across the day, these women won him over with such totality that he willingly assuaged their questions of why he wanted to go to Bethel. His unyielding claims from the morning all but silenced, he told them exactly what he thought they wanted to hear. We saw them all laughing, and we took that as a good sign. Daniel was being Daniel, and charming them in the process. Fortunately, they weren't laughing when it came to the testing portion of the interview. That wouldn't have been a good sign. We left the interview with the understanding that he would hear either way by the beginning of February. If it were a letter, it would either be a *no* or a *maybe for down the line*. But if it were a box, he would be accepted into the BUILD Program.

JOY CLINE

As we waited all over again, I began to think how very different our next year might be if Daniel went to Bethel. Christmas was upon us, and Geoff, Daniel and I headed to the movie theaters for what had become for us an annual tradition around the holidays. *A Dog's Purpose* was in the theaters at the time and was our unanimous choice. Daniel has always had a soft spot for dog movies. The premise of this particular movie was how dogs derive purpose in serving their owner's greatest need. The main story of the movie centered around a boy named Evan and his dog Bailey. Evan and Bailey grew up together and were inseparable. Bailey's purpose was companionship, and he played his role unwaveringly. But as Evan matured, he was not as faithful as his dog. His pursuit of relationships, sports, and college left a void in Bailey's one purpose in life: to provide companionship to Evan. As Hollywood is apt to do, they portrayed this in a heart-wrenching manner. While Evan is away at college, Bailey dies, seemingly of a broken heart for a lack of purpose. Evan languishes in deep regret.[9] By that point in the movie, I was sobbing, trying unsuccessfully to hide my tears from Geoff and Daniel. I was doing exactly what I always accuse Geoff of doing—putting our family into the movie. Daniel was every bit inseparable from Lizzy, and I knew Lizzy was approaching the age at which we lost Puck. The movie punctuated a deep fear in me that we could lose Lizzy while Daniel was at Bethel and how that would devastate him and sink him into deep regret. Also in the back of my mind was that the movie might further boost Daniel's defense against Bethel in his unwillingness to leave Lizzy behind, fearful of facing the same fate as Evan.

We left the theaters with all the more reason to pray. Geoff even took to enlisting the prayers of the students and teachers

---

[9] Universal Pictures Home Entertainment. (2017). *A dog's purpose*. Universal City, CA.

SPECIAL

who attended the Faith Club at his school. One morning in January, Geoff's co-worker and fellow Faith Club advisor, Tara, sheepishly sought him out. "I hesitate to share this with you in case this wasn't from the Lord," she began, "but I had a dream last night that I saw a box on your steps that was meant for Daniel. I felt I should share this with you." While at face value, this might not seem such a stretching prediction. But neither Tara nor the students knew Daniel's fate was wrapped up in a box. Geoff had never told them.

Geoff, stunned by the accuracy of her words, thanked Tara and said, "That's exactly what we're praying for. If it's a box, it means he's been accepted to Bethel." And our hopes grew a little stronger.

Yet for all our hope, the end of January came and went…no box. The first of February came and went…no box. February second…the same. But we also took comfort in that while there was no box, there also was no letter, which meant we were still in the running. On February third, I was home for the day, and you can bet I was looking for the postal worker when he pulled a box from his bag and set it on our steps. The box was not just any box, but one that bore Bethel's navy and gold emblem. I snapped a picture and sent it off to Geoff, and together we thanked God and began to let our prayer partners know Big Prayer One was a yes.

We have seen the heartfelt videos of acceptances to Bethel's BUILD Program on social media. That was decidedly not our experience. When Daniel emerged from the bus at the end of his day, there was a definite hop and a skip to his step.

JOY CLINE

His worries were little; his joy was great. He bounded up the driveway until he saw it...the box. Versed on its implications, his skip slowed to a walk. He warily eyed the box bearing his name, picked it up, gathered the remaining mail, and came inside where I met him.

"What do you have there, Daniel?"

"It's a box."

"Who's it for?"

"Me."

"Why don't you open it."

While I would have torn into it, Daniel gingerly picked away at it so that the whole unboxing was a drawn out affair, testing my patience. When, at last, its contents were revealed, he found a Bethel scarf and a letter.

"What's the letter say?"

Daniel scanned the letter and said, "Here, you can read it." I eagerly gobbled its words. The letter was from Dawn Allen, and it confirmed that Daniel had, indeed, been accepted into the BUILD Program.

"Daniel! You get to go to Bethel like Ben! You should be so proud! I'm so proud of you!" I hugged him, but he was already on the move to his after school snack and computer time, as if it were any afternoon.

For our part, Geoff and I surprisingly didn't linger long on Daniel's acceptance either, despite how much we had prayed for it. Instead, we shifted to figuring out how we might actually

SPECIAL

pay for such an endeavor. A friend of ours knew the family of a boy from a neighboring suburb to ours currently enrolled in the BUILD Program. He reached out to them to see whether they would be willing to talk to us about their Bethel experience. They agreed. What ensued was a two-hour conversation where the Jacobsons shared with us their son Joel's journey. Our desire to somehow get Daniel there only grew as they regaled Joel's campus experiences. But within our conversation, a major roadblock also emerged. Joel had a DD waiver from our county that helped the Jacobsons fund Bethel. Daniel did not have a DD waiver, and subsequent conversations with his case manager only fueled the impossibility of the timeline for securing one in time for Bethel. We were disheartened.

Yet as large as the cost of Bethel loomed over us, I think greater still in our minds was Daniel's willingness to actually acquiesce to attend there. He held the trump card in his hand, and was ready and willing to play it at whim. Even as we joyfully shared his acceptance to Bethel with others, he was quick to quip, "But it's my choice whether I go!" This was definitely a full blown mountain before us, and we urged our prayer warriors to pray harder that it might be moved. We did the same, but we also strategized.

As an accepted candidate to the BUILD Program, Daniel was invited to an overnighter at the university to experience what life might be like if he were to go to school there. We scheduled his visit to coincide with his spring break at TESA. Believing in the power of Bethel's community, we hinged our hopes on this overnight experience. While decision day for colleges is traditionally May 1st, we circled the day after Daniel's overnight for his decision on Bethel, hoping to capitalize on the experience.

JOY CLINE

When we went to drop Daniel off for his overnighter that Sunday in late March, we were greeted by Patrick, a first year student in the program. He showed Daniel where to put his stuff and escorted us all to the Dining Center for dinner. For a young man who likes his food, the Dining Center was heaven for Daniel with all of its choices and desserts. Patrick was quick to show us the ropes, and Daniel walked a little taller for having successfully navigated the labyrinth that is the cafeteria. Conversation flowed easily at the table, as we grilled the students about life at Bethel. Afterwards, we gathered Daniel's duffel bag and headed to Patrick's dorm room, where we saw there was a bed already prepared for Daniel. At that point, we got the unspoken message that it was time for us to leave, as the boys were heading off for some basketball in the gym. All evening, Geoff and I kept looking around for signs of the BUILD staff, but were surprised to find none. At first, it made us a little uncomfortable, for as much as we had riding on this experience. But the more we thought about it, the more we were impressed that this responsibility was entrusted to the students themselves, just as it would be for traditional students. On the way home, we talked about all we had seen and heard, and we committed the critical next forty-eight hours into the Lord's hands, knowing this was make it or break it time.

It was a quick turnaround for us the next day, as we made the fifty-minute trek back to Bethel in the morning for a parent orientation meeting, even as Daniel was attending classes with the BUILD students. In the meeting, we were able to connect with the parents of other admitted BUILD students. We also learned a bit more about the program.

What especially impressed us was the intentional progression towards growth and independence we saw across all aspects of the program. Students spent their first year in a traditional

SPECIAL

two-person dorm room with a common bathroom on the floor. By their second year, they moved into an apartment with a full kitchen and living area. Greater space meant greater responsibility in cleaning and cooking. In their first months at Bethel, students ate most of their meals in the Dining Center as part of their meal plan. By the end of their second year, they had greater flexibility and control over where they had their meals. Students were limited in their transportation options for leaving campus their first semester, but with success they gradually progressed to taking campus and public transportation with a simple online sign-out form that kept track of their whereabouts. First years spent much of their day in core classes with their BUILD cohort, systematically adding more and more elective classes with the larger Bethel population across their semesters. Even their employment internships shifted with time. The first year they worked at jobs around campus. But by their second year in the program, most worked off campus at jobs that paid them a competitive wage.

It was all so incredibly thought through to promote incremental growth with well defined structures of support. We could see Daniel thriving under such a protected, yet protracted, environment.

As we drove home from Bethel that afternoon, the car ride home was surprisingly quiet. I think we all had a lot to think about. Of course, we had lots of questions for Daniel about his time at Bethel. Not surprisingly, most were met with his standard "good," no matter how many ways we tried to extend the conversation. We gave him his space and told him instead what we had learned in our parent session. The big conversation about Bethel could wait until the appointed time.

The next night after dinner, the appointed time was no longer distant. It was here, and it was now, and you can bet we were

JOY CLINE

praying! We set Daniel down and asked him the question from which there was no turning back. It all started or ended with this conversation.

"We told you it was your decision, Daniel," began Geoff. "So what are you thinking about Bethel? From all you saw these last couple of days, can you see yourself there?"

Daniel was quiet for a moment, desperately mounting—it seemed—his defense. "But what about hockey?" Daniel implored. "I still want to play hockey." He had recently completed his second season between the pipes as "the guy" for the RAVE Purple Special Olympics poly hockey team. He had a lot of friends on the team, and he wanted to hold on a little tighter to the familiar as the ground shifted beneath him.

We saw the anxiety in his eyes, but we also knew the opportunity before him that could be lost if he did the safe thing and remained stagnant. Geoff and I looked at one another, and I went out on a limb, "You can still play hockey for RAVE if you go to Bethel. We'll come get you for practice and take you back afterwards." Of course, even as I said it, I knew I had stretched my authority. A fifty-minute drive there and back twice every Wednesday night through a Minnesota winter was no small commitment. I hoped I had rightly read Geoff's eyes.

Daniel mulled it over for a minute. His defenses exhausted and his will resigned, he yielded. "Okay."

Making sure we understood him correctly for the seismic shift it signaled, but also almost afraid to ask, Geoff restated, "So you want to go to Bethel?"

"Yes."

SPECIAL

Trying not to overreact and somehow cause him to retract his answer, Geoff and I played it low key in telling him what a great decision we thought that was and how proud we were of him. All the while inside, we were exploding in celebration and in wonder at the change God had orchestrated in Daniel's heart, mind, and will. But then again, why were we surprised? Isn't that what we had prayed for in Big Prayer Two?

Two down, one to go for the Big Three. We had come so far already, but now had just over a month to figure out how we might pay for this wonderful opportunity called Bethel. And we already knew the traditional route through a DD waiver would not be ours.

Coming up on our calendar was a meeting with Megan Zeilinger, the social services program coordinator for our county. Megan's job was to meet with the parents of all those graduating from Dakota County transitional programs to help coordinate services post graduation. Geoff and I had never met Megan before, but it didn't take long for us to realize we were in a bonafide power meeting. Besides Megan and us, also in attendance at our 10:00 meeting were Megan's assistant, Daniel's case manager, Callen, and his Vocational Rehabilitation Services supervisor, Kourtney.

Megan began by asking us what Daniel's plans were after graduating from TESA. Still riding the glow from Daniel's recent decision to accept Bethel's offer, we excitedly told her about the BUILD Program and our desire to see him attend. We handed her everything we had about the program, emphasizing why we believed it would be a game changer for Daniel.

She spent some time looking it over, then addressed Callen, "How is Daniel being funded after graduation?"

JOY CLINE

"He has a CEED budget," replied Callen, referring to money Daniel was allocated through the county known as Community Employment and Engaged Day.

"Here's what I want you to do, Callen. I want you to request that Daniel's CEED budget be maxed for the next two years, and I want you to write it this way…" Megan went on to detail several of the courses and services provided by the BUILD Program with the justification as to how they met the CEED budget guidelines. Callen was feverishly taking notes, trying to keep pace with Megan. "Oh, and when you're done, submit it to me." With a giggle she added, "I'm the one who approves it."

Megan next turned to Kourtney and showed her Bethel's Jobs and Employment and Internship courses' descriptions, as well as their support fee. The two went back and forth before coming to the consensus that VRS could fund those portions of Daniel's tuition.

Finally, she pondered the fee for the overnight live-in support, as well as the Social Skills course and its description. Megan asked, "What is Daniel's actual diagnosis?"

"He's DCD and autistic," I replied.

"I have an idea." Megan left the room, presumably to make a call.

She returned beaming. "Callan, I have some more work for you! Dakota County currently has an autism grant to be used for funding educational and vocational opportunities for those with autism. My good friend Ericka, who's also a Bethel alum, approves the recipients. I want you to apply for the grant on behalf of Daniel for his Social Skills course and overnight live-in support at Bethel, wording it this way…" And with that,

SPECIAL

the clock hit 11:00, and Megan wished us well and bid us goodbye. Out of the room she went, on her way to make another graduate's dreams come true.

As Geoff and I left the building, we looked at one another in disbelief and asked out loud, "What just happened?" It all went down so very fast. We were stunned from an hour's long meeting that had obliterated our final obstacle to Bethel. In our hands was our copy of the BUILD Program's financial sheet, now full of Megan's notes and computations. After all her scratchings and cross outs, all that remained for us to cover was Daniel's room, meal plan, Bible/Theology course, and activity fee. We could handle that!

We thanked God. He had made a way where there had been none. And we so clearly knew: all glory belonged to Him alone! We went out for lunch to celebrate and circled Daniel's move-in date— August 23, 2017–in prominent red ink across all our calendars. Daniel was going to Bethel!

14

GROWING PAINS

But even as August 23rd loomed large on our calendar, an unsettledness tugged at me that we weren't quite ready yet. Despite Bethel's belief in Daniel's readiness by virtue of his acceptance, we saw gaps when we tried to envision him navigating college life. Daniel still missed buttons when fastening his shirts, and he often left his pants stuck in his socks without a reminder to untuck them. He still missed spots when shaving, and was fine leaving his hair disheveled with a mere run-through of his fingers. He never did his own laundry, nor did he ever purchase anything on his own from a store or restaurant. Heck! He didn't even have his own credit card, so averse we were to putting one into the hands of one who lacked an understanding of the value of things. For in Daniel's mind, a TV cost no more than a video game or a book. Perhaps the greatest of our omissions, however, was his lack of savviness with a cell phone. In fact, Daniel didn't even have one, as all our kids were late-comers on the cell phone scene. We simply didn't see a great need for it occupying his days… until August 23rd.

What began as an unsettledness nudged me into a plan of action as I looked out on the summer of 2017 with its circled August deadline. I sat down, paper and pen in hand, and identified all of Daniel's deficiencies heading into Bethel. Fortunately for me, but maybe not so for Daniel, I had the entire summer before me to chip away at the list. I knew better than to overwhelm him with everything at once. My plan was

SPECIAL

both methodical and progressive, though my name for it said otherwise. I called it Boot Camp. Daniel called it Torture. We had him start cleaning his own bathroom. And though it meant more loads of laundry each week, we tasked Daniel with doing his own laundry as well...sorting, washing, drying, folding, and putting away—the whole shebang. It definitely would have been a lot easier and less time consuming to simply have continued doing it myself. And though my German bent towards efficiency railed against it, I knew Daniel's growth and preparedness depended on me stepping back. We got him a debit card that shared an account with Geoff and started finding opportunities for him to pull out his card from his wallet to pay for things. Knowing he would be making Target runs while at Bethel, we also showed him how to request money back from a payment so that he could have cash on hand as well.

To further his money skills, each summer afternoon after reading a book together, I worked with him on bills and coins. Sometimes I'd have him count me out an exact amount. Other times I'd have him "pay" for something from the money he had, figuring out on a calculator the change he should get back and counting that out as well. We practiced price comparisons, having him determine the best option to buy. But the one thing he never really mastered was understanding the true value of items. Fortunately for us, Daniel never spent beyond a true need, ardent rule follower that he was. We definitely knew other parents who struggled to contain their child's indiscriminate spending.

And, of course, in preparation for Bethel we also unleashed into his hands a new cell phone...well, more accurately, a hand-me-down cell phone. But hey, it was new to him! The learning curve with the phone, for the most part, wasn't steep for Daniel. He had owned an iPad for five years by then, and

JOY CLINE

there was a lot of carryover from that to his Apple phone. Our hope was to increase his ability and willingness to use his phone as a means for communication, something that would be essential to bridge the forty miles between us. To do that, I would text him a Question of the Day. Daniel would text his response back to me.

Daniel has always struggled with communication. In fact, he had an accommodation throughout high school that allowed him to type all his papers, taking full advantage of auto-correct. But even auto-correct technology couldn't mask his spelling challenges or his incomplete thoughts. And while I, as his mother, could mostly decipher his texts, I knew the staff at Bethel would struggle to do the same. I moved to Plan B and worked with Daniel to become comfortable using the Voice-to-Text feature on his phone. It frustrated him just enough to mostly revert back to typing his responses, but at least it became another option for him to be understood.

A phone now as his constant companion, we contended with another giant…social media. Daniel's app of choice was Facebook, and he spent far more time on it than we would have liked. With access to his account, we monitored chat activity to protect Daniel from unsavory "friends" who might prey on his naivety and vulnerability. We knew with the move to Bethel that while we still might have access to his account, our meaningful oversight and teachable moments would be limited by the distance. Instead, we used those final months before college to try and help Daniel discern on his own the difference between friends and "friends."

Yet despite Boot Camp and all our efforts to prepare Daniel for college, I don't believe any of us were really ready when the day dawned on August 23, 2017. Sure, our minivan was packed with such precision that another Kleenex box couldn't

SPECIAL

be shimmied in. A silence fell over us all as we mentally checked off final lists in our heads and jumped into the car. Daniel was especially edgy that morning, striking down our attempts at conversation with clipped responses. Change and the unknown pressed heavily in on him. His autistic tendencies had a way of escalating in times such as these to cope with that which he couldn't contain.

While Geoff and I had experienced the Bethel welcome once before with Ben and knew what to expect, this was new territory for Daniel; and we were about to be treated to a front row seat to it all. As we made the turn into Bethel, we were met by a lineup of cars. Slowly inching our way up to the familiar orangish-brown mosaic brick entrance that marked our arrival, we were stopped and given a piece of paper to put on our dashboard bearing Daniel's name and Nelson 216, his new home for the next nine months.

But before we could log our final mile to his new home, we were stopped one last time. As we rolled down our window, we heard distant eruptions of cheers and booming music with a throbbing bass. Bethel President Jay Barnes and his wife Barb peered into the passenger window to warmly greet Daniel and welcome him "home" to Bethel.

Pleasantries aside, we snaked our way in a parade of cars ever closer to Nelson Hall, the same dorm, coincidentally, we had come to five years earlier with Ben. The music and cheers grew increasingly louder. By the time the dorm finally came into view, we gazed in astonishment as we watched an energetic crew of dancing, singing, and cheering students direct the car in front of us into its final paces and then completely engulf it. While the new student inside was escorted into the dorm, the rest of the crew made short, cheerful work of emptying the car of its cargo in a matter of minutes.

JOY CLINE

By this time, Daniel's eyes were wide open. And I believe he was a bit mortified that his turn was next for this over-the-top welcome. But his anxiety was momentary, as a student popped her head into the window and said, "Welcome to Bethel, Daniel! Come on, let's get you your room key and get you signed up for your Homecoming shirt!"

"Okay" was Daniel's subdued response; but even so, I could feel his resistance melting away in the invitation and sense of belonging. Dodging the students converging on our van, he and I fell in line behind our guide and mounted the steps to Nelson. By the time we reached Nelson 216, the room was already filled with all of Daniel's belongings. As I surveyed the room, I hadn't remembered the rooms being quite so small. We began unpacking our bins, hoping to clear a space before his roommate got there with all of his stuff. On Daniel's desk were Bethel promotions announcing upcoming events across campus and a handful of cards from his new housing mentors. As one who has always been our mail guy, Daniel flipped through them all, his smile widening.

I looked at my watch…nearly 10:00. We had just over an hour and a half to bring some semblance of order to this chaos before our orientation luncheon. The task before us seemed daunting.

Into this chaos stepped Tyler—Daniel's new roommate, his mom, and stepdad. Daniel and Tyler were not completely new to one another. They had run into one another unexpectedly a few weeks earlier while on campus for meetings. They had also communicated a little back and forth on Facebook. The most important piece they exchanged was to find they were both sports fanatics…a good start. In that vein, Tyler came bearing a gift for his new roommate—a Minnesota Wild lanyard. Daniel snapped his new room key onto it and flung it around his neck.

SPECIAL

"Thanks."

There were now six of us in the room, each with our own agenda, even as the minutes ticked away. The room constricted in on us all as we sought to empty bins and clear them away from the room just as quickly for breathing space. We also navigated multiple preferential decisions between Daniel and Tyler to create a common space they both felt good about. Knowing the weight of the day for two autistic young men, Geoff and I tried to keep the mood light. Even Tyler began cracking jokes to dispel the stress that permeated the room. But time was our enemy and with little of it, tensions remained simmering. Hands flew and bins were tossed. Geoff was on constant bin removal and trash duty by this point. We knew anything left unpacked would probably remain so until our next extended return to Bethel weeks away. We wanted to bring as much order to that dorm room as we possibly could for Daniel's sake. After all, this was his first stretch of any significant time away from home. His room had to be a refuge for him amidst all the change.

"Hey," said Geoff, interrupting my rampage and Daniel's desk organization. "I think we better stop and head over to

JOY CLINE

orientation now. It's 11:20." I threw Daniel's quilt and pillow on his lofted bed and plopped Georgie and Binks on top for good measure. I'm sure Tyler scratched his head at the sight of them. They would be a conversation for the days to come. I surveyed the room one last time before closing the door. It would have to do.

After the morning's rush, it felt good to finally sit down and rest. We joined Tyler and his parents at a table near the front. As if sensing our pent-up stress, BUILD Director Dawn Allen welcomed us warmly, "You made it!" She exclaimed in a reassuring tone. "Now take a deep breath, and know you've got this. It's why you were chosen to come to Bethel. We believe in you! And when you doubt yourself, look around this room. You have a whole lot of people here who will step in to support you, not the least of which is the Lord Himself. But after all that unpacking, you must be hungry. Let me say a quick prayer, and let's get you something to eat."

We all had a turn through the catered buffet and after some time connecting without the duress of unpacking, we settled in for our introduction to the BUILD Program. Much of what we heard that day was of the practical nature, preparing us all—at least to the extent they could—for what we might expect in the days ahead.

"Mistakes will happen," warned Dawn. Then, surprisingly, she added, "You *want* those mistakes to happen, because real growth happens when we learn from our failures."

Before the students left the luncheon for additional orientation sessions with the larger university, each of them was given a shirt bearing the letters BU. "We selected these shirts especially for you," said Dawn, "as a reminder that here at Bethel University, we want you to feel comfortable and safe

SPECIAL

to B-U (be you)." I couldn't help thinking about Georgie and Binks nestled on Daniel's bed back in his dorm room. And with that, Daniel and the other twelve that made up BUILD's newest, Cohort Three, left the room clutching their new shirts and ready to take on Bethel.

Most of the rest of the BUILD staff joined the students as they left, but Dawn remained to finalize details and provide an opportunity for any questions we might still have. After a protracted explanation of the safety and security measures in place at Bethel and—in particular—with the BUILD Program, one dad raised his hand and asked, "But what are the safeguards in place to ensure my daughter doesn't just walk off campus?"

Dawn looked steadily at him and said, "We have carefully studied the school records and background of your student, and don't believe her to be a risk here at Bethel. If you are concerned, then I think we need to have a conversation after this meeting about your child's readiness for Bethel." It was the first time I had heard her raise a stern voice, but I liked her response. As one taxed with the burden of always selling her program, Dawn's honest, straightforward answer endeared me to her as one who would speak truth. She didn't sugarcoat things.

The meeting was coming to an end, yet Dawn gave us some parting words of advice,"Don't be alarmed if a week goes by, and you don't hear from your son or daughter. We're keeping them very busy, and they're learning to be college students apart from you."

Geoff looked at me and said, "A week? I think Daniel would be hard pressed to make it a day!"

JOY CLINE

"It's been quite a day, Moms and Dads," continued Dawn. "Let go now and release your grip on your student, knowing we'll be their safety net."

Our drive home that afternoon was much like our ride up to Bethel that morning—quiet, with each of us alone in our thoughts. At times we commented on events from the day or raised concerns about things forgotten or left unsaid. We were emotionally and physically drained, yet somehow the tears remained at bay.

We would make the eighty-mile round trip to Bethel a couple more times in the coming days for meetings and such, but our time with Daniel was limited while he raced through the exhilarating, yet exhausting rituals of Welcome Week. Our final chance to see him before classes started was at Bethel's Commissioning Service, where we, as parents, were given the opportunity to worship together and pray over the school year for our children. As if to foreshadow the type of service it would be, we were handed a packet of Kleenex at the door. I scoffed at the cheesy gesture as I stuffed them away in my pocket.

Music has always spoken profoundly to me in some of my deepest times of crying out to God. This moment was to be no exception. As I sat in Benson Great Hall, my heart grappled with stepping back and letting go of Daniel, even as I looked out at him a couple of rows ahead of me in the auditorium sitting with his new friends. I knew the bumps ahead were sure to come. A life with Daniel had taught me to expect those. Yet in that moment, all that was in me wanted to shield him from them as I had his entire life. For I was a mother who had—in

SPECIAL

Daniel's vulnerability—been mothering my son far longer than most.

Into that moment, those Kleenex now in hand as I dabbed away the tears, God spoke to me at my core the truth of who He is with the worship team's leading of the song, "King of My Heart."[10] The lyrics drummed: "You are good, good, oh, oh." With each tolling of those words, the truth struck deeper that I *could* entrust Daniel into God's more-than-capable hands. I had a lifetime of evidence of His goodness and faithfulness, even in getting Daniel to this very moment. I resolved to claim this faithfulness to protect and grow him in the days ahead. I had to trust God, I had to trust the BUILD staff, and I had to trust Bethel. The song droned on: "You're never gonna let, never gonna let me down." Into that solemnity of that moment and claiming the song's reassurance, I laid my son at His feet and took a step back. And I cried some more. Those Kleenex I had so quickly dismissed at their pocketing were certainly coming in handy now!

I eventually managed to pull myself together before the service's ending. We met Daniel afterwards for a moment to hug him, tell him we loved him and would be praying for him. He was quick to pull away; after all, he was a college student now.

"Give us a call Monday night," I added, verging on begging. "Let us know how your first day of classes went. Love you!" And with that, we left him. But this time, it was with an air of finality.

The emotions aside, Geoff and I settled into life without Daniel living at home. Lizzy was definitely the winner here. Sure, the

---

[10] Google. (n.d.). Google search. https://www.google.com/search?q=king%2Bo f%2Bmy%2Bheart%2Blyrics&ie=UTF-8&oe=UTF-8&hl=en-us&client=safari

JOY CLINE

house was quieter, and Geoff and I shifted fairly easily into the whole empty-nester thing—a stage of life we never expected to be ours. But while we were settling in, Daniel was encountering some of those bumps on the road to independence.

It began fairly innocently. After a week and a half or so of classes, he had somehow misplaced his student ID. At Bethel, your student ID is everything. It gets you into your dorm, and it gets you your food. Daniel loves his food. As such, he wasn't going to survive long without his ID. Motivated by his growling stomach, he sought out help from the BUILD staff to get it replaced. A stop at the Office of Safety and Security with a fresh $5 surcharge on his account, and Daniel was back in the Dining Center line clutching his new ID card.

Within a week, however, he had lost his ID yet again. But this time, along with it, he had also lost his debit card. Both were housed in his badge holder that had inexplicably detached from his lanyard and wasn't showing up in the Lost and Found. The BUILD staff stepped into action again, helping Daniel to problem solve the *why's* behind his missing badge. They ended up going with him to the Campus Store to purchase a new, more secure badge holder to safeguard him from another loss. Of course, Daniel had to alert us about the debit card so we could stop payment on it and get another one quickly in the works. He struggled to tell us. His text, even in its typical difficulty to decode, circled around without landing his admission. Daniel was trying fiercely to be independent.

A week or so later, my phone rang. As I raced to retrieve and answer it, I saw it was Daniel. I looked at my watch…2:15. It was an unusual time for him to call. "Hey, Daniel! What's up?"

SPECIAL

"Hi…." His voice trailed off and there was an awkward pause. In the background I could hear Janelle's voice offering him talking points. "I lost my key," he said finally.

"Your key?"

"To my room. I lost it. I have to get a new one."

At that point Janelle got on his phone to clarify. "Hi, Joy. This is Janelle. Hey, I just wanted to let you know that to make a new key for Daniel's room, Bethel charges $50 to his account. Are you okay with that?" I assured her we were. "Moving forward, we think we have this figured out. We gave him a clip to attach to his lanyard that should hold the new key more securely." I thanked her as she passed the phone back to Daniel.

"It's okay, Buddy," I reassured him. "These things happen. You'll get this figured out…hopefully that new clip will help!"

For my part, I tried to sound upbeat. I tried to be patient and grace-filled. These were the very mistakes Dawn had talked about only a few weeks earlier. We were just awaiting the growth shoot—maybe something like *two* weeks without losing something—that might signal the mistakes had finally hit their mark. It seems something did indeed click. For Daniel not only didn't lose anything in the next two weeks, but it would be well over a year before anything turned up missing again.

September was nearing its end, and another marker of growth for Daniel was quickly approaching…his 22nd birthday. As his mom, I was fretting. We had pledged to ourselves that we would leave Daniel on campus until fall break in October…seven long Daniel-less weeks. We bought into Dawn's challenge that to do so would hasten his attachment to the Bethel community.

133

JOY CLINE

Not wanting to cave, we wrestled with how we could make the day special without the comfort and familiarity of birthdays past spent celebrating at home.

Moving to Plan B, Geoff and I decided to bring the birthday to Daniel. We pulled together all of his favorites—Domino's pizza, Caesar salad, pink 3-level confetti cake, Pepsi, Lizzy, Mary, his best pal Jake, presents—all loaded into the car. While the weather was a bit nippy and gray, we scooped Daniel up from his dorm and unloaded the party at a nearby park.

Knowing Daniel's penchants for not tooting his own horn, so to speak, I struggled with the hard truth that Daniel might go through his birthday without anyone even knowing or acknowledging its significance at Bethel. That thought grieved me as a mom. So I went to the local Dollar Tree, loaded up on birthday decorations, and decorated the door to Daniel's dorm room before we went to the park. Yes, I was that mom. But I found I needn't have worried. Daniel had made enough new Facebook "friends" at Bethel that his birthday didn't go by unrecognized. And, of course, the BUILD staff marked the day with a card and gift of a free drink at the Royal Grounds, Bethel's on-campus coffee hangout. My momma's heart glowed in gratitude.

Another familiarity of importance to Daniel during that fall stretch was football Sundays. Without a television in his room, I wondered how he would watch his beloved Packers. Complicating matters was the fact that he was, after all, deep in Vikings territory. Again, I found I needn't have worried. Daniel quickly identified his Nelson Packer faithful by their team jerseys on game days. They packed the Shack, Nelson's lounge, each televised Packers' game. Packers' fans were everywhere! Even his BUILD cohort was split roughly down the middle between the Vikings and Packers in their football

SPECIAL

allegiances, offering him plenty of buddies to hang with on game days.

One evening when Daniel was returning to Bethel from an off-campus activity, he came upon a startling scene outside Nelson. Several campus security cars, local police squad cars, and an ambulance were parked on the dorm courtyard, lights flashing, along with a crowd of onlookers. Police tape blocked the main entrance to the dorm, relegating Daniel to a side entrance to reach his room. When Daniel reached the second floor, he encountered more police tape down the hall from his room. It was eerily quiet that night for a floor full of freshmen guys. Daniel would learn later from BUILD housing mentors that one of his non-BUILD floor mates had taken his life in his dorm room earlier that evening while Daniel was away. He was one of Daniel's Packer buddies who joined him in the Shack on game days. The BUILD staff offered counseling as the students tried to come to grips with this loss that seemed so senseless and so personal. And in the heaviness of that night and the days to follow, the idea of a college education took on a whole new meaning.

We leaned heavily on Daniel's housing mentors through those days of shock and confusion. By now, their names had become familiar to us: John M., John C., and Tanner. They were a constant in Daniel's new life, and we heard their names pop up frequently in our conversations with him. As Bethel students themselves, the housing mentors were well versed to guide the young men of BUILD's Cohort 3 in the nuances of campus life. I remember seeing this in action during Welcome Week, as the mentors familiarized the new BUILD students with the Bethel campus. The students were right there with them in lock step as they raced through a myriad of campus activities. And I realized just how we, as parents, were quickly becoming irrelevant in the shadow of these housing mentors' attention. The mentors ascertained what made each of the boys tick and connected with them on that level. They became all-access contacts for the students through this monumental life transition, intentionally typing their numbers into each of the boys' cell phones.

But as the weeks went by, they became so much more than mere phone contacts. This threesome led the boys in activities, sometimes as simple as hanging out and playing Mario Kart in their room. Other times, they organized outings to the movies or a Timberwolves professional basketball game. They became the overseers to some of the BUILD students' independent living skills, inspecting their laundry and rooms on a weekly basis. Daniel especially anticipated the nightly check-in from the housing mentor on duty. It became, for him, the Bethel equivalent to a home tuck-in. Yet first and foremost, John M., John C., and Tanner were brothers in Christ. They modeled Jesus to these first-year BUILD students by corralling them for Sunday night Vespers, a weekly worship service on campus, and in encouraging them to attend Wednesday night Shift Bible studies with them.

SPECIAL

Hardest of all, the housing mentors served on the front lines of conflict resolution. Sure, the residential supervisors stepped in when matters took on a more serious tone. And even Dawn herself met with the more challenging cases. But as the ones living a couple of doors down, the housing mentors were in the trenches with a proximity we would come to appreciate.

As we neared Thanksgiving break, we began to receive ripples that all was not right. Tyler messaged me that Daniel was copying him and some of the other BUILD students. I thanked Tyler for telling me and told him that everyone has areas they are trying to improve. Copying was Daniel's area, and he had been working on it for some time. I told him I was glad Daniel was at Bethel where they live out the BUILD program's verse, 1 Thessalonians 5:11a: "Encourage one another and BUILD each other up."[11] And while I tried to put a good face on it, this interchange saddened me. I thought we were past Daniel's copying days. I called Daniel that night and, without implicating Tyler, tried to help him recognize his copying and others' distaste for it.

A month went by, and we heard nothing. I began to hope this had merely been an isolated incident, and Daniel had righted the ship. But then one day, right before Christmas, we heard from Tyler again. He was having "concerns" about Daniel's copying again, this time in regards to one particular classmate. He described an incident from class that day where Daniel had antagonized this other student with his incessant copying of her. He just wouldn't let up, according to Tyler. For his part, Tyler felt it was his place to stand up for this girl and let me know. I was heartbroken. Tyler cast a light on Daniel that we hadn't seen in our visits to campus. The larger Bethel

---

[11] *Bible gateway passage: 1 thessalonians 5:11 - new international version.* Bible Gateway. (n.d.-a). https://www.biblegateway.com/passage/?search=1+thessalonians+5%3A11&version=NIV

JOY CLINE

community widely embraced Daniel, but it seemed he was struggling at times with his BUILD classmates.

It was with this message that I knew I needed to take another big step back as a mom. I couldn't facilitate this conflict from a distance. It wasn't my place. I needed help.

I typed a response to Tyler, encouraging him to reach out to the housing mentors with his concerns. They were right there to assist Daniel and him through this together. Tyler thanked me and assured me he would do just that. It was into that backdrop that I received a phone call a few days later.

"Hi Joy, this is Dawn. Is this an okay time for you?" I assured her it was. "I want to run something by you and get your thoughts. David Kaetterhenry has been living by himself all semester and has expressed a desire to have a roommate. We have seen that David and Daniel have developed a beautiful friendship and wondered if you would be open to having Daniel move in with David after Christmas break."

I hesitated, collecting my thoughts. I recalled Dawn's famous words from orientation: "You *want* those mistakes to happen, because real growth happens when we learn from our failures." I bought into her words...totally. I wanted to see Daniel grow, and I wasn't so sure removing him from the situation would accomplish that.

"I don't know, Dawn. He's pretty comfortable where he's at, and change is never easy. Besides, I think it's been good for Daniel to have to learn to adjust to living with Tyler. Maybe he should just stay."

"Oh, but David could *really* benefit from having a roommate. He's very social, and his parents have been wanting him to

SPECIAL

have someone to share his room with. David has even said his roommate *has* to be a Packers fan, and that he'd like that Packers fan to be Daniel."

Something in her tone and insistence….and suddenly, I got it. Dawn wasn't really talking about David, as much as she was about Tyler and Daniel. She had been in the trenches with this conflict herself, it seemed, and had found a creative solution that would benefit all. I knew when to throw in the towel.

"Sure," I said. "Let's do this." And so, even as we packed up Daniel's things for a long Christmas break, we also packed up his room and moved it across the hall and five doors down to room 226. It would be a fresh start for everyone.

15

GOOD AS GOLD

And so when we returned back to campus in January, it was to room 226 that we dropped off Daniel and his laundry, not 216. David, his new roommate, hadn't arrived yet. To be sure, we would know when he did. You usually heard David before you saw him, so large his voice and so inextinguishable his spirit. He came bounding into every situation, full throttle energy and uncontainable joy.

"Buddyo!" David exclaimed from the stairwell. Then bursting into the room, "Buddyo! You're here, and we get to room together!" For full effect, he lifted Daniel up off the floor in a big bear hug. Daniel just giggled, as he plopped him back to the floor.

By then David's dad, Kevin, had joined us in the room, and David and Daniel had fallen into breaking down the weekend's Packers loss to the Lions as we rearranged the room to fit two. In his interaction with David, Daniel wasn't being told how to do something or not do something. He was simply talking football with a friend. There was a mutuality to their relationship.

Perhaps a change of scenery *would* be good after all—a place where Daniel was able to, in Dawn's words, "B-U." Daniel was certainly feeling the love. His and David's happy chatter warmed me.

SPECIAL

Daniel and David had actually met years earlier at a state Special Olympics swimming meet, though neither would remember it. They happened to land on the podium together, and a live picture I shot captured a connection that was apparent even then. Besides the Packers, it seemed the two of them shared many mutual interests: food, choir, *Boy Meets World* reruns, playing the guitar, swimming, and pursuing Jesus. These mutual interests would bond them together for the remainder of their days at Bethel.

The BUILD Program encourages the students to get involved on campus. Daniel found his niche in two activities: choir and swimming. Both wove him into the larger fabric of Bethel.

Participating in choir was a natural fit for Daniel after his high school years. He joined a mixed choir assembled exclusively for Bethel's big Festival of Christmas production. Daniel loves singing and loves Christmas music. He had been in the audience many times over the years to watch Ben perform. This would be his turn, and it would be a memorable highlight to his year.

But when the night of the performance arrived, Festival of Christmas became memorable in ways we wish we could have forgotten. It began normally enough. Geoff and I picked up Mary along the way with a car full of food. We had planned to have dinner at Geoff's dad's house before making our way to Bethel. Daniel loved his grandpa, or "Gramps," as he liked to call him. Theirs was a relationship sealed over baseball, fishing, and time together at the cabin. Gramps never thought too highly of himself. He could laugh at his mistakes, deriding himself with a familiar "Morrie!" We never understood the reference. But in his own mistakes, Daniel giggled and let out his own, "Morrie!" Mistakes lost their punch with laughter as part of the equation. Compassionate and protective man

JOY CLINE

that he was, I believe Daniel's disability especially endeared him to Gramps. He loved Daniel, and Daniel loved him. Daniel couldn't wait to perform on the big stage for Gramps!

When we arrived at Gramps' house, however, all was not right. He was slurring his words and experiencing dizziness and double vision. Past experience taught us he was having one of his TIAs, or transient ischemic attacks,[12] which temporarily blocked blood flow and caused a mini stroke. But the TIAs also put him at high risk for suffering a full-on stroke. We helped him out to his car, and Geoff drove off with him to the hospital with urgency.

With their departure, a heaviness settled over the night. Mary and I ate dinner alone, packed up, and headed for Bethel where we met Ben and one of his friends. Finding our seats, we realized we had purchased handicapped seating to accommodate Gramps. Now we felt a little self conscious in occupying them without him. It would be the first of many moments in the evening where we felt the weight of his absence.

As music is apt to do, the singing swept us away into the joy of the Christmas season; but it was short-lived. I began receiving text updates from Geoff. The news was not promising. Gramp's TIAs in the past, while scary, had always ended with him being discharged from the hospital within a day. This episode, it seemed, had taken a decidedly worse turn. One message, in particular, jolted me: "The doctors said he might not make it through the night."

---

[12] Mayo Foundation for Medical Education and Research. (2023, April 14). *Ministroke vs. regular stroke: What's the difference?* Mayo Clinic. https://www.mayoclinic.org/diseases-conditions/transient-ischemic-attack/expert-answers/mini-stroke/faq-20058390

SPECIAL

"Might not make it through the night?" I passed my phone to Mary and Ben who absorbed the news in silence. Festival of Christmas was reduced to background music as my mind chased down the ramifications of these words and how I would communicate this all to Daniel as he came bounding to the lobby afterwards to be celebrated under Gramp's proud gaze.

At the concert's end, Daniel's happy trot slowed as he approached us. "Where's Gramps? Where's Dad?" He asked, taking a quick survey of the crowded lobby.

When I told him about Gramps having to go to the hospital, Daniel just nodded his head, but kept smiling. Daniel always smiled. Of course, I didn't reveal the gravity of the night and the real possibility of Gramps not living through it. I didn't want to heap any more on what should have been a celebratory night for him. But thankfully, we didn't have to ever go there. Gramps did indeed make it through the night and was released from the hospital about a week later...definitely weakened, but home for Christmas. We rejoiced.

The other activity Daniel joined on campus was swimming. At Bethel, swimming was a club sport. Without a pool of their own, the club had to rent time at nearby Hamline University for their biweekly practices. As the only BUILD student joining the club that year, Daniel was embraced by the rest of the team, who always sought him out and made sure he had a ride to practice. We thanked them with gift cards to Kwik Trip.

JOY CLINE

It was no surprise that Daniel joined the swim club as one of his activities. He has always loved the water and felt in it a sense of release. It's the reason we escaped to indoor water parks as a family when we were fed up with Minnesota winters. It's the reason we always made sure any hotel we were staying at had a pool. What *was* a surprise, however, was just how little we knew about Daniel's swim club escapades. As a student-led campus activity and not BUILD-driven, we were dependent on Daniel to fill in the gaps of communication, and he kept his cards pretty close to his chest.

One Saturday afternoon we called Daniel for a check-in. "I had a swim meet today," he announced without fanfare.

"You did!" I exclaimed. "Where was it?" Geoff and I were a little dismayed at not being informed earlier so that we could have seen him in action.

"Minnetonka...by Uncle Joey's. We went by his house." My brother did indeed live in Minnetonka, and the Minnetonka Aquatics Center was at Minnetonka Middle School East, a stone's throw from his house. I was impressed that Daniel recognized the familiar setting despite the lack of context.

"What did you swim, and how did you do?" And with those questions, we realized we had met our limit. "Good," was his one and only response. We couldn't pry any additional details out of him.

About a month later, Daniel called us all excited because he had another swim meet coming up—the last one of the year—and this one was going to be an overnighter. They were staying in a hotel.

SPECIAL

"Really? Wow! That's awesome, Daniel! Where's the swim meet going to be?" I asked, hoping again for an invitation to come watch him.

"Minnetonka," he replied.

An overnighter? In Minnetonka? Maybe Minnetonka is just the spot for these collegiate swim club meets, I thought. Minnetonka was only a thirty-minute drive from campus… hardly overnighter status. But I surmised it was, perhaps, the club's way of celebrating the season's end. I tried to extract more details with the idea that maybe we could just show up at the meet, but none were forthcoming.

The day of the meet, I happened to pull up Find my Friends, only to find "my friend" Daniel in Wisconsin, traveling along Interstate 94 East. Showing Geoff, we began to follow his progress across the state. With all the intrigue of OJ Simpson's famous highway heist, we wondered where this might end up. When he reached Milwaukee and it became apparent that this was his landing spot, we called him.

"Hey Buddy," I said. "How's Minnetonka?" Daniel was quiet.

"I think," continued Geoff, "that if you look out your window, right about now, you'll see the Milwaukee Brewers stadium."

"Yea," Daniel replied with a little chuckle. He was busted.

Minnetonka? Milwaukee? What's the difference? They both start with "M."

There was great wisdom for keeping your student on campus on weekends for experiences such as these. Daniel kept plenty busy! If there weren't BUILD activities, there were larger campus events to attend. Daniel was especially partial to any of the events that included food, movies, or sports. Of course, Bethel had plenty of those! Football Saturdays were particularly epic, but Daniel would also go to basketball, hockey, soccer, and softball games. It was all in who you knew, and Daniel had developed a lot of relationships with the athletes. He knew who they were playing each week and put them through their paces in talking through the opponent.

Besides going to assorted Bethel sporting events, Daniel also participated on Bethel's Special Olympics Unified bowling and basketball teams. As a unified sports club, traditional students from Bethel played alongside their BUILD teammates in both area and state competitions. For his part, Daniel was thrilled to be joined in the arena of competition with those he saw in the hallways of Bethel. His first year bowling, his partner was Justin, a fellow freshman who lived down the hall from him in Nelson and who was always one to stop and chat with us when we visited. His second year, Daniel was paired with Ryan, who also led the unified basketball squad. Ryan had a natural rapport with Daniel. I was to find later that he volunteered to lead a Young Life Capernaum group for mentally disabled youth. It didn't surprise me. Ryan cheered and laughed and encouraged Daniel all the way to a gold medal. And when I went to thank him later for his stellar performance, he just shrugged and said, "Daniel was the one who carried us today. Did you see his strikes?!"

Of course, Daniel was also participating in poly hockey with his Special Olympics team back at home. We had kept our end of the bargain and were faithfully picking him up for practices back in Apple Valley every Wednesday from November through February. Most Wednesdays I would make the afternoon trip to get Daniel, we'd all have dinner together, and then he'd go to practice with Geoff who would return him to Bethel. It became our weekly six-hour circle that we came to treasure, even in the cold, dark, and unpredictability of a Minnesota winter. I especially loved having Daniel's rapt attention for the commute. He hopped in the car fairly bubbling over with all the news he could pack into a fifty-minute drive. This was decidedly not the boy I had dropped off at Bethel in August, a boy content in himself and in the silence. Daniel's new life was full, and he couldn't wait to share every aspect of it. The change was stark.

One of the things I most appreciate about the BUILD Program was all the ways it required Daniel to stand on his own two feet. We weren't there, ready and willing, to rescue him from any and every situation. He had to sink or swim. At his previous transitional program, he had worked on many of the same employment and independent living skills. However, when he got on the bus at the end of the day and came home, they

JOY CLINE

were mostly forgotten. In the isolation of how they were taught, the skills lacked the transfer to everyday life.

But at Bethel, the living and working skills he acquired in the classroom were readily put into practice in the dorms and in his internships. He did laundry, cleaned his room, shopped, and learned both the soft and hard skills of holding down a job. Housing and job mentors provided oversight to help guide, encourage, and hold Daniel accountable. And in the repetition of it all, he gained confidence. So much so that when he came home on breaks and I tried to pick up old established ways of doing things around the house for him, Daniel called me off. "You don't need to help me. I can do this."

I was learning, just as much as Daniel. But unlike Daniel who was learning to step into things, my learning was to take a step back. One area, in particular, remained elusive for me. While hockey night commutes revealed huge strides in Daniel's ability to carry conversations, I readily fell into old patterns when we were with other people.

One night when Daniel was home and we were walking Lizzy, one of our neighbors stopped us to chat. Marlis wanted Daniel to tell her all about Bethel. He answered her questions until he didn't have anything else to say. But Marlis wanted more, and Daniel gave me that look—that look that has always said, "Rescue me!" I started to oblige, but then Marlis interrupted me.

"Why are you looking at your mom, Dan?! *You* tell me." Marlis was a retired para who had worked in the school with students such as Daniel. She wasn't going to let him off the hook. The Daniel who didn't think he had anymore to say, found something deeper within him. And I had an epiphany moment. It seems Bethel was teaching me a little something too— teaching me to keep my mouth shut so Daniel could find his

SPECIAL

voice. People often want to hear what Daniel has to say more than what I say anyway.

Daniel had ample opportunities to test his emerging voice. His first job internship at Bethel was as a tour guide for any prospective BUILD Program candidates. Besides guiding students and their families around Bethel, Daniel also prepared informational folders and manned the information desk. He loved all aspects of the job. In middle school and high school, Daniel thrilled for his dash through the hallways between classes, fitting in as many interactions as possible. Here at Bethel, it was his *job* to command the hallways...how could life be any better?

But somehow it was. To accompany Daniel through the halls was to be invisible to his star power. He knew everyone, and they seemingly knew him. They shouted out his name and raised their hands to fist bump him. They stopped simply to connect with him. He had come full circle. Even as he had been the prospective student just a year earlier and had looked admiringly to Maggie, here he was doing the same for the next cohort of BUILD students.

In their interactions, it wasn't hard to see that the Bethel community largely embraced the BUILD students. Most recognized the huge challenge it was for these mentally handicapped young adults to be college students. They were both their cheerleaders and helpers on this journey, whether in the dorm, dining center, classroom, or football stadium. Greater still, as Christians, the Bethel students were compelled by a higher calling: "Love the Lord your God with all your heart and with all your soul and with all your mind and with all your strength. The second is this: 'Love your neighbor as yourself.' There is no commandment greater

JOY CLINE

than these."—Mark 12:30-31[13] The BUILD students were their neighbors at Bethel. In loving them, the students of Bethel were fulfilling Jesus' command.

But a funny thing happened along the way...the traditional students witnessed an indomitable spirit and determination in seeing the BUILD students push through hard things, and push through them with such vulnerability. I believe as much as the BUILD students grew in their tenure at Bethel, equally so the traditional students grew in valuing their disabled peers as equals, as fellow children of God on this journey called life. A perspective, no doubt, they will carry on in life to their future homes, work places, churches, and communities.

Within such a fertile community and with Daniel a prime recipient of attention through his job as tour guide, it wasn't long before we began to hear murmurings from some of the other BUILD parents. "Golden Boy," they began to call Daniel. And on the outside, I had to admit, Daniel's time at Bethel looked pretty "golden." But it wasn't perfect. I knew the behind-the-scenes Daniel...the lost items, the incessant copying, the insecurities, the challenges.

One of the hardest days for Daniel occurred just as he was wrapping up his first year at Bethel and preparing to move back home for the summer. I was subbing that day in a Spanish class, proctoring a test, when my phone rang. It was Dawn. Unable to answer, I had to let it go to voicemail. Moments later, Geoff was able to receive her call.

"Hello, Geoff, this is Dawn Allen. I'm calling to let you know there was an incident today at Bethel involving Daniel." With

---

[13] *Bible gateway passage: Mark 12:30-31 - new international version.* Bible Gateway. (n.d.-b). https://www.biblegateway.com/passage/?search=Mark+12%3 A30-31&version=NIV

SPECIAL

that, she proceeded to recount an encounter in the dining center. Apparently Daniel and several of his BUILD cohort were having breakfast together when Daniel fell into copying one of the girls. Exasperated, she asked him to stop. When he pleaded innocent and continued to copy her, Tyler took things into his own hands. He had had enough. He walloped Daniel. The dining center fell into a hush, so unaccustomed it was to a fight within its walls. I believe Daniel was just as startled as those around him who had witnessed the hit. Both boys were quickly escorted out of the dining center and into the BUILD office where Dawn would attempt to simmer high emotions.

"Now we sent Daniel to the nurse, and he checked out just fine," reassured Dawn, "but I wanted to let you know." She paused and added, "I also wanted to see if you wanted to press charges against Tyler."

Press charges? The seriousness of the matter settled over Geoff. Still stunned, he managed to mumble, "No…no charges necessary." Geoff and I have been marriage mentors at our church for years. We know that in nearly every argument, it takes two. So while we could never justify a physical altercation, we equally knew that a year's worth of pent-up frustration was behind it. Daniel had just pushed Tyler's buttons one too many times.

Dawn continued, "Tyler has been suspended for the final days of the semester. He is packing up his room and will be leaving campus this evening."

When Geoff got home from school that afternoon, he filled in the gaps from his conversation with Dawn. It made me so sad. I especially hurt for Daniel. I could only imagine the hit's larger impact on his self esteem…to have it happen in such a public space as the dining center. We FaceTimed him that evening,

JOY CLINE

but he clearly didn't want to talk about the incident. The day had cast a sadness over him as well. I sensed a tentativeness and a fidgeting to him. He assured us he was fine, but it seemed he had been taken down a notch or two.

In the days that followed, we were to find healing. Dawn initiated the healing process by bringing Tyler to the luncheon marking the year's end, where he offered a sincere apology not only to Daniel, but also to the larger group. Daniel broke the silence first, "I forgive you, Tyler." And the rest of the BUILD community followed in behind him in offering their forgiveness as well. It was a beautiful moment of reconciliation and restoration. In the retelling of that moment, I was never more thankful that Daniel was at Bethel, where Jesus' example of forgiveness could be sought and extended.

But the healing was incomplete. I felt a nudging in me to reach out to Tyler.

"Tyler," I wrote, "I just wanted to touch base with you about yesterday. Geoff and I are both teachers, and we fully understand all conflict is the result of two people, not one." I continued, "Mostly, Tyler, we want you to be able to look us in the eyes next year, confident there is no ill will from us. We are in Daniel's corner; we are in your corner, as we are in the corner of ALL the BUILD students, desiring to see you built up in unity and succeeding to your very best. It's why we sent Daniel to Bethel, and it's why your parents sent you to Bethel—to grow and be shaped. Sometimes it's the hardest days that do the best shaping and growing, and yesterday was one of those 'hardest' days. Geoff and I are praying God uses the difficulty of yesterday to shape and grow you and Daniel towards a better tomorrow. Have a great summer, Tyler! We'll look forward to seeing you on move-in day, when we'll look you straight in the eye with smiles on our faces!"

SPECIAL

Tyler thanked me and asked if I might call his mom as well. Apparently, she was none too happy with him. When I called, Jennifer was beside herself. "We didn't raise Tyler that way," she intimated. I reassured her, as well, that we understood that conflict is the result of two people, not one. We were ready to put this behind us, and we wanted *her* to be able to look us in the eye without thought of condemnation. We both hung up with a mutual understanding and a gratitude for BUILD's role in the healing.

The "Golden Boy" had definitely lost a bit of his sheen in the school year's ending, but there remained a glimmer to build on. Certainly the fires of the final days had taken their toll. But the funny thing about gold is that when it's heated in the fiery furnaces, its impurities rise to the top, enabling them to be skimmed off. What remains is pure gold. Impurities aside, we couldn't wait for what year two of Bethel would bring!

"In all this you greatly rejoice, though now for a little while you may have had to suffer grief in all kinds of trials. These have come so that the proven genuineness of your faith—of greater worth than gold, which perishes even though refined by fire—may result in praise, glory and honor when Jesus Christ is revealed."[14]

---

[14] *Bible gateway passage: 1 peter 1:6-7 - new international version.* Bible Gateway. (n.d.-a). https://www.biblegateway.com/passage/?search=1+Peter+1%3A6-7&version=NIV

16

STRETCHING

We returned to Bethel in the late summer without the anxieties of the unknown that had hung over us the previous summer. The car brimmed with excitement, as Daniel and I drove up together. Geoff followed behind, as it now took two cars worth of stuff to settle Daniel into his second year. The challenges of the previous year, particularly at year's end, were nearly forgotten in the hope of a fresh start. As if to emphasize this, as we made the turn into Bethel that day, my playlist serendipitously queued up "Confidence" by Sanctus Real, but we called it "The Daniel and David Song:"

> I'm not a warrior, I'm too afraid to lose
> I feel unqualified for what you're callin' me to
> But Lord with your strength, I've got no excuse
> 'Cause broken people are exactly who you use
>
> So give me faith like Daniel in the lion's den
> Give me hope like Moses in the wilderness
> Give me a heart like David, Lord be my defense
> So I can face my giants with confidence[15]

The song seemed so appropriate for our welcome back to Bethel. I smiled at the Lord knowing just what I needed to remind me He was in the details. To be sure, year two would still have its "giants." But I also knew with God's equipping,

---

[15] Google. (n.d.-a). Google search. https://www.google.com/search?q=confidence%2B by%2Bsanctus%2Breal%2Blyrics&ie=UTF-8&oe=UTF-8&hl=en-us&client=safari

Daniel had a year behind him of slaying them and notching some confidence in the process.

Year two of the BUILD Program also had some sweet upgrades, namely a shift from the two-person dorm room to a full apartment overlooking Lake Valentine. The apartment even had air conditioning, a welcome addition after last year's blistering late summer heat without it. Daniel thought he had died and gone to heaven with all that cool space.

When we arrived at North Village, Daniel's new home for the next nine months, the welcome was much more subdued than it had been the previous year. Still, there were ample hands on deck, ready and waiting to help make quick work of emptying our cars.

David and Daniel would once again be roommates this year. It was a match that stuck. Arms full, we found the door to their apartment already unlocked and opened. A sign on the door christened the apartment: "Warning: Man Cave, Enter at your own risk." We decided to take our chances and stepped inside.

JOY CLINE

A blast of cool air met us. David had obviously discovered the air conditioner and was giving it a whirl. The novelty would take some time to wear off after last year's heat. We were immediately struck by the spaciousness of the boys' new apartment. There was definitely room to stretch out. And unlike last year, six adults fit comfortably into the space. Heck! We could each have our own room! The apartment sported a full kitchen and dining area, a living room, a bedroom the boys would share, and a full bathroom. We all busied ourselves with unpacking and putting the boys' mark on the space. You can bet there was plenty of Packer memorabilia being slapped up on the walls and shelves. It was truly a "man cave!"

It wasn't long before we heard a knock at the door. It was Tyler, who had already moved into his apartment a couple of floors up. I was thankful I had tackled the hard conversations with Tyler and his mom last spring. Tyler had no apprehensions at showing up at David and Daniel's door. There was no awkwardness. There was no drama. I looked him straight in the eye, no gaze averted, and smiled. "Welcome back, Tyler. Are you ready for year two?"

"You better believe it!" He chimed. God had had His healing ways.

SPECIAL

We were to learn that with all the perks of being second year students in the BUILD Program, also came the expectation of greater responsibility. Certainly, the very reason the boys had moved into their apartments before the return of most other Bethel students was so they could mentor the incoming first-year BUILD students as they settled into campus life. The bar was set higher when it came to their independent living skills as well. Now they had an entire apartment to clean and maintain. They also had a kitchen at their disposal, providing greater cooking and shopping opportunities. David, who aspired to be a sous chef, was especially excited to set up the kitchen and begin cooking his masterpieces.

Sometimes Daniel lived up to the higher expectations of year two, while other times he fell short. One weekend, not long into their arrival back to Bethel, Daniel and David were relishing their newfound freedom. The next thing you knew, David was buck naked, and Daniel was taking pictures of him in the nude and sending them off to one of their new housing mentors, Kadrien. As is possible with young adults with mental disabilities, it was some horse play without thought of the larger implications and deeper consequences.

On Monday, Daniel was summoned to Dawn's office where he was confronted with his actions. He was given no leeway because of his disability. This was a serious matter that could have had even farther-reaching ramifications had he posted the pictures on social media. He would not be let off lightly. Daniel's residence hall director, Nick, emailed us the details of the night, along with Bethel's response. Daniel was placed on probation with the understanding that if he had another disciplinary incident, he would be suspended from Bethel, possibly even expelled. When Geoff and I read those words, our hearts sank. There was a lot of year left, and the prospect of Daniel keeping his record clear of another indiscretionary

JOY CLINE

action seemed daunting. Suddenly, the "Golden Boy" wasn't looking so golden anymore, though few were aware anything had happened. David would later step up and admit that the whole episode had been his idea, yet it didn't excuse Daniel from his lack of judgment in taking and sending the picture.

We were quick to respond to Dawn and Nick, lending our support. Our hope was that the gravity of his actions would sink in for Daniel, that he would grow. "Have at him," we said, hoping a united front would hasten that growth. It wouldn't be the last time the boys made bad choices. Yet always ringing in the back of my mind were Dawn's words, "You *want* mistakes to happen, because real growth happens when we learn from our failures." I trusted the process.

Another area in year two where Daniel gained greater autonomy was in his ability to get off campus for excursions. Sure, he still had to sign out on a Google form so the BUILD staff knew where he was when he left campus. This was a safety standard that spanned his time at Bethel. But now he was no longer restricted in his movements or limited with whom he could leave campus. Most times, Daniel took the Bethel shuttle. He never strayed far…maybe to Target or Rosedale Mall. On occasion, Daniel and David were invited off campus to the apartment of friends from Bethel. It might be for a football game, movie, video games, or simply to hang out. These invites followed on the heels of one student's standing invitation for breakfast together in the dining center every Monday. It became known as Mondays with Chloe. Bethel students earnestly knocked down walls to inclusion, embracing the apostle Paul's words in 1 Corinthians 12:27: "Now you are the body of Christ, and each one of you is a part of it."[16]

---

[16] *Bible gateway passage: 1 corinthians 12:27 - new international version.* Bible Gateway. (n.d.-a). https://www.biblegateway.com/passage/?search=1+Corinthians+12%3A27&version=NIV

SPECIAL

With such examples, it wasn't long before David and Daniel caught the vision. One of their big inspirations was to host a Super Bowl party. While they had high hopes in the planning that their Green Bay Packers would be playing in it, they had to content themselves in planning for the commercials with the game serving as the subtitle. Of course, Chef David planned the menu, but Daniel also contributed. It wasn't polished and the clean-up lingered, but dorm friends showed up to watch the game with them and they were empowered by their hosting prowess.

Sometimes such confidence overshot their judgment. With a full kitchen at their disposal, the boys made a steady diet of bacon and eggs, as evidence of their expanding waistlines. And once, David undercooked some chicken, landing him back home battling food poisoning. Fortunately for Daniel, he hadn't eaten any of the chicken. He was still a little leery of chicken from his mysterious illness episodes and had declined it. As for David, he did indeed recover, a little wiser for the wear.

Soon it seemed you hardly saw one without the other. Where there was Daniel, there was David; and where there was David, there was Daniel. They were silly together, David serving as the prankster. He would find little hideaways around Bethel, and jump out to scare others with a booming, "Aaaaaarrrgh!" Daniel played his part, ensuring that laughter followed them wherever they went. Their joy and abandonment were contagious. I think Bethel undergrads secretly looked wistfully at the twosome, so unencumbered they appeared from the cares of this world. It was hard not to smile when they were around. As this friendship deepened, Daniel took great security in it. His copying ways, so prevalent his first year at Bethel, began to diminish, almost disappearing altogether. Here was a friend

JOY CLINE

who accepted him simply for who he was. David was good for Daniel.

While the choir the boys had sung in together their first year had since disbanded, they found other ways to be together. David joined Daniel on the swim club their second year at Bethel. With the two of them in tow, I'm pretty sure every practice turned into a pool party. Perhaps that was the team's undoing, because that year there were no swim meets—no trips to Minnetonka or "Minnetonka." That was probably just as well. I think the boys found their time in the pool more unwinding than strenuous.

In a surprise move, Daniel decided not to play poly hockey his final year at Bethel. Geoff and I could hardly believe it! The commitment on which attending Bethel once hinged had become a side note. We took this as a good sign. Daniel was digging in at Bethel and finding his place there. And while we would miss our Wednesday dinners and car rides together, we definitely would not miss the drives across the metro into the teeth of a Minnesota winter.

For his part, Daniel threw himself into his final year at Bethel. He once again joined the unified bowling and basketball teams. He also took guitar lessons. Playing the guitar had long been a passion of Daniel's. He began playing while still in middle school. And while I say "playing," I use the term lightly, as there were no chords involved and the strumming could be inconsistent and loud. Still, Daniel "played" with gusto and passion. Pity those living next door to Daniel!

When Daniel was choosing his elective courses for his final semester at Bethel, one of the options was to take music lessons. His eyes lit up. Here was a boy who had been dragged along to Mary's and Ben's piano lessons, not to mention their

SPECIAL

trumpet and saxophone lessons, for nearly his entire life. How could we deny him this opportunity? We said yes. Though it cost us a pretty penny and we held few expectations from it, we beamed when he picked out "Mary Had a Little Lamb" on his guitar, with all the focus and concentration he could muster. As a parent of a special needs child, sometimes it's the small milestones that are most meaningful.

Although David also played the guitar—enough to truly earn the word "played"—his parents chose not to enroll him in lessons. He was devastated. Not recognizing how hurt he was at missing out on lessons, Geoff and I saw him quietly retreat to the bedroom to brood when we talked about the guitar lessons. This would be one of those times when there was a Daniel, but not a David, and it had opened a wound.

As part of that "greater independence, greater responsibility" piece that came with being a second-year student in the BUILD Program, job internships took on an added dimension. Completely relegated to being on campus their first year, internships in the second year of the program were mostly off campus and paid. While Daniel still served as a mentor tour guide to the new incoming first-year students from time to time, he also had moved on to other internships.

One of those new internships was as a volunteer playologist at the Minnesota Children's Museum in St. Paul on Saturdays. Daniel's job as a playologist was to engage children in different exhibits, showing them how to navigate them and encouraging participation. As the son of two teachers, it seemed a good fit. Besides, Daniel had really always been a kid at heart. Joining him on Saturdays was his job mentor, Logan, a sophomore at Bethel. Logan drove Daniel to his internship and was there on site to help Daniel be a better playologist. But Logan was so much more than that. He became a friend to Daniel, sometimes

JOY CLINE

celebrating the end of a shift with a lunch out or joining him in the dining center during the school day for a meal.

Daniel was also employed at Target for its seasonal push. He trained at what was then a new concept—the self-checkout lanes. His job was to greet customers as they came and went, and offer assistance when they encountered problems in checking out. Mostly, he helped them through weighing produce and buzzed for help when he was stumped. It was a sweet gig, though it did require us to cut short our Christmas vacation to run him up to Shoreview for his shifts over the break. Daniel was learning a little something about real life: you don't always get to choose your hours, especially when you're a seasonal employee.

Following his seasonal stint at Target, Daniel became a bagger at the Roseville Lunds and Byerly's supermarket chain. He learned to pack groceries and became a natural at customer relations, flashing them his smile.

Besides being well paid for his internships, Daniel was also compensated in other ways. As a parting gift from all his time as a tour guide, Daniel was given a Bethel football game jersey from Admissions. It even had helmet scuffs and a small rip boasting its authenticity. He treasured that jersey. On more than one occasion, he was saved by tips he received bagging groceries to fund appetizers and movies with friends. Ever so slowly, Daniel was learning the value of hard work.

During the final semester, the focus of the Independent Living Skills class shifted to prepare Daniel and the rest of Cohort Three for life after Bethel. They explored relationships, marriage, and children. The class was taught by Lisa Bjork, BUILD's new assistant director, who had replaced Janelle Kelly in the fall. Despite having big shoes to fill, Lisa quickly

SPECIAL

stepped into her new role at Bethel, winning the students with her genuineness. It was clear this was way more than just a job to her. She showed up to cheer on her students at Special Olympics unified basketball tournaments and joined them at chapel. Like Dawn and Janelle, she had a heart for the students, and it showed in her daily interactions.

One day after a particularly rousing class discussion on marriage, I received a text from a concerned David. "Hi this is David kaetterhenry here in our class he dose not want kids and he said he is not getting a wife what should I do to help him." David could not conceive a life without marriage and a family, yet his Buddyo was obviously just fine without one. His level of concern to reach out to me in an effort to "help" Daniel both warmed and amused me.

As talks such as these began to frequent those final months, we saw an emerging trend. Daniel was becoming increasingly preoccupied with his graduation date. He'd say, "On May 25th, I'm going to come home and live with you, Dad, and Lizzy..." And then he'd add for emphasis, "FOREVER!" We found his preoccupation with May 25th a little puzzling, as we knew he was having the time of his life at Bethel. Living back at home with Geoff and me would definitely be a downgrade by comparison. His insistence at a future back in Farmington also unsettled us, as we had looked at his time at Bethel as a launching pad for a life of independence. He certainly had gained the skills and confidence for just that, but it seemed the heart and will were still lacking.

Before we knew it, that much anticipated date of May 25th was upon us, and we once again found ourselves journeying through a series of lasts. The first "last" during graduation week was the BUILD celebration luncheon. A new tradition had been established that year whereby a BUILD staff member

JOY CLINE

honored each of the graduates. Lisa, who had developed a special bond with Daniel in her first year on the job, was the one to recognize him. In the honoring, she spoke a Scripture and word over him that perfectly encapsulated Daniel. She chose Colossians 3:12: "Therefore, as God's chosen people, holy and dearly loved, clothe yourselves with compassion, kindness, humility, gentleness and patience."[17]

"Daniel," Lisa began, "the word that comes to mind for you is kindness. You make a point of discovering what is dear to others and intentionally reminding them of those things. That is a rare and wonderful gift! On a daily basis, we have seen you making meaningful, personal connections with those around you. Your thirst for Jesus and worshiping Him in chapel, Vespers, or in your daily interactions is beautiful. We are so proud of all your accomplishments in college, Daniel. Your innate, God given kindness will serve you and those you know well. Congratulations on your graduation, Daniel. Keep spreading your kindness!"

It was a powerful word spoken over Daniel that he took to heart. I knew behind those words was the connection Daniel had made to Lisa's favorite song in chapel, "What a Beautiful Name." Daniel was quick to tell her whenever he heard the song, even sending her a video of the song one weekend to lift her. As wonderful and upbuilding as Lisa's words were, they wouldn't be the last acknowledgement of the week.

President Jay Barnes, who had welcomed Daniel to Bethel his first day on campus with the words "welcome home," now knew him by name as one of the Bethel family. He used the platform of the Royal Reception dinner for graduates and their

---

[17] *Bible gateway passage: Colossians 3:12 - new international version.* Bible Gateway. (n.d.-d). https://www.biblegateway.com/passage/?search=Colossians+3%3A12&version=NIV

SPECIAL

families to give Daniel a shoutout. "Daniel, your smile lights up the halls of Bethel." His words were unexpected and settled in our hearts.

After the dinner, we attended the Baccalaureate service, where the graduates were given a Bible and a Bethel serving towel as a reminder to follow Jesus' example of serving those around them, even as He had humbly washed his disciples' feet before the Last Supper. As Daniel and David walked across the stage to receive communion one last time and collect their gifts, I saw the meaningful interactions Lisa had spoken of—both on stage and off—the laughter, the hugs, the conversations that came easily. When you've spent much of a lifetime seeing your son be underestimated and undervalued, the gestures of the Bethel community that evening overwhelmed me. I lost it. I was sitting next to Lori Kaetterhenry, David's mom, my emotions raw. As I failed to contain my sobs, I looked to Lori and blubbered, "They loved our boys." And she nodded in agreement, her eyes brimming with tears as well.

The next day, Daniel's highly anticipated May 25th finally did indeed dawn. Geoff and I got to Bethel in plenty of time to claim seats and ensure Daniel was all set. We had decided against bringing Gramps with us to the ceremony, as navigating the crowds, distances, and long day seemed daunting. Gramps was too proud for a wheelchair.

Arriving at North Village, we found Daniel and David attired in their robes and ready to go. Geoff finalized the look by knotting Daniel's tie for him. But when we summoned the boys to the car, they declined the ride. Daniel and David wanted the campus shuttle to take them the final mile to their graduation meeting spot. Long-time driver, Hans, obliged and would have the honor of depositing the boys at the Robertson Center.

Mary, Ben, and Allison joined us in Benson Great Hall, though Allison and Ben would be dividing allegiances. Allison's sister, Amy, would be graduating in the same ceremony as Daniel. As we settled in, the dignitaries and speakers took their turn on stage. Our ears perked up when the student commencement speaker highlighted fist bumps from Daniel Cline as "one of the best parts of the Bethel experience."

Fifteen BUILD students started in the fall of 2017, and eleven remained to walk across the stage and collect their Certificate of Applied Studies that day. Each got to shake President Barnes' hand and claim the piece of paper that represented a journey of highs and lows, accomplishments and failures, but undoubtedly confidence and growth. Much like Mary, Jesus' mother, who marveled at her blossoming twelve-year-old Son, I "treasured up all these things and pondered them in my heart."[18] It was a wonderful ending to two years that had changed the trajectory of Daniel's life. That glass ceiling that had been imposed at the age of nine with the words from Farmington's Director of Special Education—"He'll be lucky if he can read street signs"—suddenly broke open to a future that seemed bright and untethered.

---

[18] *Bible gateway passage: Luke 2:19 - new international version.* Bible Gateway. (n.d.-e). https://www.biblegateway.com/passage/?search=Luke+2%3A19&version=NIV

SPECIAL

Though anticlimactic from all the day's festivities, our family found one of the better burger joints in the Twin Cities to celebrate Daniel. We picked up Gramps en route; and under his proud gaze, we toasted Daniel. Gramps made sure not to miss this moment.

But our journey at Bethel wasn't quite yet over, for what remained was the clearing out and cleaning up of "the man cave"...a daunting task indeed. For while the boys had weekly cleaned their apartment under the oversight of their housing mentors, there remained a deep cleansing that now fell on our collective shoulders if we were to secure our housing deposit—high motivation. The Kaetterhenrys and Clines divvied up the chores to tackle this monstrosity, with the clock ticking on our unbudging checkout time of 11:45. Much like our entrance to Bethel twenty-one months earlier, hands were flying and trash was exiting. I had the dubious assignment of cleaning out the kitchen—a filthy task. At one point, in search of trash bags, I found some at the bottom of the boys' trash bin. But I was to find something more. As I pulled out all the bags laying waste in the bin, I came upon one near the bottom that wasn't quite empty. Curious, I opened it to see a package of raw chicken obviously well past its prime. Of course, as immediate as its sight was its putrid smell. Retching, I snatched it shut, double bagging it and knotting it for good measure. Arm stretched as far away from me as possible, I handed it off to Daniel with the urgent instructions, "Run! Now! Throw this away!" And out the door he flew! The journey had not been perfect, but it was memorable.

As we latched the door shut one final time, removing the "man cave" sign, the final vestige to mark Daniel and David's time at Bethel, we hugged one another and vowed to maintain contact. We drove away with Dr. Seuss' famous words coming to mind: "Don't cry because it's over, smile because it happened."[19] Oh, but we were smiling! And now, Daniel was coming home "to live with Mom, Dad, and Lizzy...FOREVER!"

---

[19] Signupgenius. (2024, November 6). *30 seussisms to inspire you.* SignUpGenius. https://www.signupgenius.com/School/dr-seuss-quotes.cfm

17

A FAITH ALL HIS OWN

To be sure, that seed planted at Vacation Bible School with eight-year-old Daniel's profession of faith had not remained dormant all these years. Daniel had a heart that continued to lean towards Jesus. He defied the early obstacles that had shut him out of church and sprouted ever upward.

As a homeschool family, we brought Jesus into our home and our schooling. We began our days with prayer and ended them the same. We read the Bible together and stocked our bookshelves with books that edified. We made a steady diet of *Veggie Tale* videos on movie nights and employed *The Family Night Tool Chest* for devotions. And we worshiped together as a family.

It was the latter, perhaps, that resonated most for Daniel. I had a guitar and was able to strum out a few songs. In the early days, it most often fell to action songs like "I'm in the Lord's Army," "Go, Go, Joshua!," and—Daniel's personal favorite— "Daniel in the Lion's Den." As the kids grew older, we sang current worship songs and hymns from church. Whatever the time, whatever the season, Daniel loved to worship. He eagerly joined Mary and Ben in marching around the living room belting out songs, giggling all the while.

But I think in all of this I failed to recognize the allure it was to Daniel to actually *be* the one making the music. He watched his siblings play their instruments and longed for his own

JOY CLINE

musical outlet. He loved it when he got a recorder in his fourth grade music class, but it was the guitar that always captivated him. It was what he saw up front during worship at church. It was who he wanted to be. In fifth grade choir, he actually made his own two-stringed guitar. Daniel strummed away at that guitar until it could be strummed no longer, strings finally broken beyond repair.

One morning when I went to collect my guitar for worship, I found it snapped at the neck, the result of too much tension applied. It didn't take long to identify the culprit. Daniel was testing his guitar-playing prowess when he discovered the tuning pegs. He tightened them to such a degree that the guitar simply succumbed to the tension. While I was disheartened at the loss of my guitar, it was hard to fault Daniel for his yearning and curiosity.

I never replaced my guitar, but its loss prompted a gift idea. We bought a student-sized guitar for Daniel's 14th birthday. He was giddy. At the time, one of his favorite things to do was to listen to his His Kids radio, a WiFi radio that broadcast Christian children's programming and music. Sometimes he'd follow stories from *Adventures in Odyssey* or *Paws and Tales*, while other times he'd catch a message from Pastor Mark or *Karen and Kids.* Now with a guitar in hand, he "played" and sang right along with the music, often fashioning a microphone from whatever he could find. In his mind, he *was* the worship leader. Daniel had plenty of incredible examples over the years to emulate: John Holtze from our early days at Woodcrest, and Pastors Jeff Kerr and Ryan Williams from River Valley. All were extremely patient with a young boy who idolized them, studying their technique and every move. And he was good at executing those moves! He was particularly skillful at impersonating Pastor Ryan, elevating to his tip toes and

SPECIAL

swinging his guitar for emphasis. What he saw, he copied, and brought into his own worship.

But they were patient in other ways as well. Pastor Jeff regularly fielded Facebook messages from Daniel, never tiring of his questions. Pastor Ryan and Daniel bonded over Detroit Tigers baseball, weekly breaking down the teams' on field exploits. Even our lead pastor, Pastor Rob Ketterling, recognized Daniel's passion, both in faith and baseball. He invited Geoff and Daniel to join him and his oldest son, Connor, at a Twins game.

With an upbringing and connections such as these, Daniel's faith chugged along. But it was a faith dictated far too much by Geoff's and my faith. We chose his church and small group. We constructed a lifestyle that kept him on the straight and narrow way. We even influenced the very relationships he formed, surrounding him with extensions of our own larger circles. Would his faith stand when stripped of the scaffolding we had so carefully crafted? As his first time living away from home, attending Bethel was the litmus test.

Reflecting on Ben's college experience, Geoff and I trusted Bethel and its community to nurture his brother Daniel's faith. One of the greatest facets of Bethel is the role faith plays in all aspects of campus life. As a Baptist university, it is unapologetically Christian. In fact, Bethel requires a statement of faith in its application process. But faith runs much deeper than a mere check of the box at this school. It's in the weekly gathering of the community at Chapel and Vesper services. It's in the Wednesday night Shift Bible studies in the dorms. It's in the opportunities to serve locally, and in missions stateside and abroad. It's in the intentionality to weave prayer into the

JOY CLINE

classroom and everyday life. And it's in the hallways, across the thousands of interactions that happen naturally with Jesus at the center of them. Daniel would experience it all in his thirst for Jesus.

Providing oversight to this community of faith is the Office of Christian Formation. It became one of Daniel's favorite stops in his days at Bethel. The office had three pastors on its staff during his tenure there: Pastor Laurel Bunker, Pastor Matt Runyon, and Pastor Jason Steffenhagen. All would become intimately acquainted with Daniel.

Pastor Laurel was the lead teaching pastor for Bethel's Chapel services. She was distinguishable by her ever-present high heels and her sermons that were equally as pointed. Her messages challenged the Bethel community out of complacency and into an active faith. Her messages sought unity and racial equity. Her messages painted pictures of her own stories of failure and redemption. Whatever the topic, whatever the series, the students showed up when Pastor Laurel was in the house, and that included Daniel. In fact, he never missed a Chapel, and he expected the same of others. As Pastor Laurel put it, to miss Chapel was to have to explain your absence to Daniel Cline...an uncomfortable conversation indeed. Usually, it was just easier to show up.

Throughout his college days, Daniel often found his way to Pastor Laurel's office. Maybe it was the Pepsi that Pastor Laurel slipped to him from time to time on his way out the door, but I like to think it was the comfort and safety he found within those walls, the freedom to be unequivocally him.

Pastor Matt's office was another of Daniel's regular stops. As a fellow Packers fan and an avid baseball guy, there was a natural connection. When together, the two talked football

SPECIAL

and baseball, but Pastor Matt always managed to take the conversation higher and deeper with Daniel. He had a gift for connecting with others. His official position at Bethel was to facilitate outreach and missions. Daniel would come under that leadership as he prepared for his own missions trip, and Geoff and I would serve alongside Pastor Matt on the BUILD Advisory Committee for years. Whenever Pastor Matt asked about Daniel, he would quickly follow it up with "I love that guy!" I think the feeling was mutual.

Pastor Jason was Daniel's professor for his Old Testament and New Testament classes at Bethel. He led Cohort Three with such fun and energy that Daniel would be quoted as saying, "Jason has pizazz!" Pastor Jason wove stories of his family and kids into his teaching that made the Scriptures all the more relevant and alive for the BUILD students.

At Chapel Daniel was a front row sort-of-guy, most often with David beside him, along with other assorted BUILD students and staff. He joined in singing lustily, sometimes even raising his hands in worship. Before long, others took notice of his devotion. The pastoral staff extended an invitation to Daniel to come behind stage before Chapel for prayer. Sometimes he merely joined in, while other times they nudged him to lead. They had recognized a young man leaning in and coaxed something more out of him.

Of course we were clueless to Daniel's burgeoning role at Chapel. Never one to toot his own horn, he kept us in the dark. One day a good friend of ours, Jake Vanada, was speaking at Chapel. Imagine his surprise when he stepped in for prayer. "Daniel!" Jake exclaimed. He would call us that night to divulge his encounter with Daniel at Bethel. We would also learn that Daniel had earned a new moniker—Pastor Daniel—a name that would stick.

JOY CLINE

Besides attending Chapel three days a week, Daniel rarely missed Vespers. Vespers was a Sunday evening gathering at Bethel, student-led and centered entirely around worship. It was so popular, even to a larger Twin Cities' audience, that they held two services to accommodate the overflow. Daniel and David ate dinner and headed to Benson Great Hall where they camped out—an hour early—to claim their vaunted front row seating. They didn't want to miss a single minute of praising Jesus.

For Daniel, however, his faith ran deeper than merely leaning in for worship. In the fall of his second year at Bethel, he made the decision to apply to go on a mission trip over his spring break. Unusually, he would be the only one from his BUILD cohort to apply that year. Every spring Bethel sends students out to various locations to serve God alongside missionaries through Solidarity Missions Partnerships (SMP). Daniel's trip would take him and five of his fellow Bethel students to Northfork, West Virginia, where they would work with the Bertram family as part of their Mustard Seeds & Mountains ministry. While there he would paint, help with a children's outreach ministry, and hit the roads of this Appalachian community to assist needy people through projects and companionship.

While Mary and Ben had gone on several mission trips throughout their middle and high school years, Geoff and I never imagined a context for Daniel doing the same. Few would assume the responsibility and risk of a disabled student. We always figured we'd one day go on a mission trip through River Valley and bring Daniel along with us. It blew our minds to think that at Bethel, Daniel could have such an opportunity as this unleashed from us. I think he kind of liked it as well. Part of his highlight was the long drive to West Virginia all together as a team, building camaraderie over conversations and John Denver's "Country Roads" on repeat. It was in another hotel

SPECIAL

stay without his mom and dad in sight. And it was in not seeing himself as the needy one, but in doing something for someone else who could use a leg up. Daniel returned from that trip with a great sense of accomplishment and fulfillment.

But it took the larger Bethel community to make this opportunity possible for Daniel. It started at the top with Pastor Matt, having the vision for the powerful witness of disabled students looking beyond being served to being the servers. It took the BUILD Program establishing safeguards and structures of support to make it possible. It took buy-in from fellow students on the trip to accommodate Daniel and his pace. And it involved the willingness of Kadrian, Daniel's housing mentor, to take on double duty in overseeing his needs. He sacrificed more than all, including his sleep, to integrate Daniel into the mission. He would later regale us with his attempts to beat Daniel to bed, only to fail and find sleep elusive because of Daniel's heavy snoring.

Stripped of our oversight and influence, Daniel's faith did indeed stand the test of Bethel, and—even more importantly—became his own, constructed on experiences where he showed

JOY CLINE

up, leaned in, and stepped up to serve. But all too soon, his Bethel days were over; and a persistent virus would take hold of the world, sweeping us all into a season of isolation.

Covid challenged us all on so many levels. But for newly graduated Daniel, it sliced deepest in cutting him off from the communal worship with others. It would be just over a year before we returned to church in person. It was a time that tested all of our resolves. Yet for all the destructiveness associated with the Covid years, a life preserver emerged for Daniel in the rise of online church services and social media devotionals. He was buoyed by the new access he had to church services from around the world. He streamed Hastings' Cornerstone Church on Wednesday nights. Thursday was his "preaching and worshiping night," where he followed Cornerstone online kids programming. Saturday afternoons we'd all "attend" River Valley's online service.

Not surprising, Sundays were especially full. Daniel would stream Homestead Church, Stillwater Evangelical Free Church, Hosanna Church, and Tangier International Protestant Church, where a friend of ours was pastor. More often, Daniel's streaming preferences were guided by associations he had made over the years, but sometimes his choices defied understanding.

Beyond Sundays, Daniel redeemed his increasing time on Facebook during Covid by following daily devotions from various churches. He thrilled to hear them call out his name in live feeds. It was the interaction he longed for in a shut-up world. Hosanna even recognized his loyalty by mailing him a coffee mug. He'd raise his prized cup for all to see. For one for whom transportation will always be an obstacle, the rise of the online church has been nothing short of a lifeline for Daniel.

SPECIAL

In my house I have a large collection of assorted house plants. They breathe life into our cold Minnesota winters with their green that defies the snow and cold at their doorstep. One characteristic that all my plants share is their propensity to stretch towards the sun. They will bend until they are fairly toppling over just to catch more of its life-giving rays, particularly in winter's deep darkness. Similarly, I've seen Daniel, in his unquenchable thirst for more of Jesus, bend towards the Son, especially in Covid's dark days. His faith, expressed in song and devotion, is a beautiful thing. To think it might have been snuffed if not for those stalwarts along the way who not only saw value and worth in Daniel, but also the potential for faith in him, and nurtured it.

18

ANOTHER WAY TO WORSHIP

After a trip to Disney World to mark his graduation from Bethel, Daniel slipped easily into home's rhythms. At Bethel, nearly every minute of his waking hours were accounted for, particularly his second year. Now he looked off into a future void of the structure of either work or school, and he basked in the vastness of it. No wonder he wanted to come home after Bethel "and live with Mom, Dad, and Lizzy... FOREVER." It was easy. It was comfortable.

It didn't take long before we realized Daniel was becoming a bit *too* comfortable. His days fell into an endless routine of radio programs, video games, reading, television, and baseball broadcasts. To counter, we heeded Dawn's advice and charged him with doing his laundry, cleaning his bathroom, mowing the lawn, and planning and preparing our Sunday dinners—something to give a purpose and shape to his days, something to keep his independent living skills being stretched. We wanted to keep the mighty momentum of Bethel rolling!

But a larger piece of keeping that mighty momentum rolling for Daniel was getting him working and living on his own. Those in the disability community differ in their opinions on whether it's best to first secure a job and then seek housing near it, or to find housing first and then look for jobs in the area. As the easier of the two, we chose to lock up work first. Geoff and I felt

SPECIAL

Daniel was highly marketable due to his varied and successful internships while at Bethel. The greater hurdle for him, in our eyes, was transportation. Farmington was an outermost ring suburb that fell beyond the Twin City metro transit routes. Now living at home, Daniel's options for employment shrank to a two-mile radius he could walk or bike to from our home. Add to that the obstacle of limited employers willing to hire a mentally disabled worker, and our search was looking more and more daunting.

Daniel's first job, even before going off to Bethel, was as an activities aide at Trinity Care Center, a nursing home just a short bike ride from our home. Daniel began there as a volunteer during his high school years and Joy Lauterbach, the Activities Director at Trinity, spotted some leadership qualities in him. As she put it, "He stuck out." She was quick to hire him when we approached her. It didn't hurt that we came bearing an incentive-laden promise from Dakota County to fund a good portion of his salary. So the summer before Daniel began at Bethel, the two of us rode over to Trinity a few times a week. We gathered the residents for activities, assisted them as needed, then returned them to their rooms afterwards, and generally just interacted with them.

One of the favorite activities amongst the residents was BINGO. After several rounds of BINGO with them each week, helping them mark their cards and handing out prizes, it wasn't long before we knew all their names and idiosyncrasies. We grew to have favorites and tried to make the day a little more cheery for those who decidedly weren't our favorites.

JOY CLINE

Daniel loved all the interactions. He found what was important to each resident and connected with them there. He laughed with them and learned not to rustle the feathers of the grumpy ones. Our lives became so entwined with the residents that summer that Daniel would often talk about the residents even when we weren't at Trinity. The hard part of Trinity was not knowing whether the residents would make it to our next activity. Death notices were posted on a wall near the nurse's station. Daniel's first stop at Trinity was always the wall. He's never been comfortable with death.

As we surveyed the post-Bethel employment landscape before us, our first pursuit led us back to Joy's door at Trinity. It had been a great experience for Daniel, though it did expose his limitations. When tasked with actually leading an activity, I had to step in and be pretty heavy-handed to keep things afloat. Joy recognized this and proposed a paired job for Daniel and me. Not quite ready to give up my substitute teaching days to accommodate Daniel's employment, I prayed over it for a few days and declined.

But we didn't close the door on Trinity just yet. Its proximity to our home begged for a second chance. So Geoff and I put our heads together and ventured a few doors down the hall from Joy to Matt Pomroy's office, Director of Human Resources. We floated the idea of Daniel working as a dietary aide, delivering meals to residents unable to make it to the dining area. Matt was not opposed to the idea; but as we awaited his decision, I grew increasingly uncomfortable with the life and death consequences of a mistake by Daniel. In his quest to appease a resident's wishes, could he be coerced to retrieve a restricted food or drink that could lead to a medical emergency? In his people pleasing way, I couldn't say with certainty he wouldn't. We reluctantly closed the door on Trinity and expanded the job search to communities beyond

SPECIAL

Farmington, all the while uncertain just how we might finagle transportation.

Our Plan B was to tap into Daniel's most recent Bethel internship as a bagger for Lunds and Byerly's. Lunds and Byerly's is a grocery chain known for its propensity to hire the disabled. It seemed a good fit, and Daniel agreed. He had liked all the interactions Lunds and Byerly's afforded him while bagging customer's groceries. He liked the tips. The trade-off was that the closest store was a twenty-five minute drive from our home. Increasingly becoming more desperate, we were willing to make it happen for Daniel, just to get him working.

Geoff and I figured Daniel was a shoo-in for a job there. After all, he had just finished a four-month stint working at a different location, and came vetted and trained. Heck, even the Human Resources rep, Sue Paar, who was also one of Daniel's references, said she would call ahead and put in a good word for him. Overconfidence consumed us as we entered the Burnsville Lunds and Byerly's store that afternoon on a cold call. Daniel was dressed the part and had his fresh, updated resume from Bethel in hand. We had done some cursory coaching of Daniel prior to leaving home, but felt assured that with his experience, it was a mere formality.

Just inside the doors, we found an employee and asked if we might speak to the manager. The manager seemed a bit preoccupied that afternoon, but willingly gave audience to our pitch. I nudged Daniel.

"Hi, my name is Daniel Cline." He stretched out his hand to shake the manager's. "I'd like to work at Lunds and Byerly's." He handed him his resume, and Geoff and I nodded our heads in approval. So far, so good.

JOY CLINE

The manager gave his resume a quick glance and said, "We just had a hiring fair last week."

Nodding his head up and down, Daniel didn't know how to respond. Geoff rescued him. "Daniel just graduated from Bethel as part of the BUILD Program. This past spring he had a job at the Lunds and Byerly's store in Roseville as a bagger, and he really liked working there. We were hoping you might have a position open where he could naturally transition to the Burnsville store." Pausing, he threw out his trump card, "Sue from Human Resources in Roseville said she was going to reach out to you."

"Hmmmmmmmm," the manager replied, "I haven't heard from Sue." Then turning to Daniel, he asked, "How many hours a week would you like to work?"

"I don't know...two?" I cringed. Daniel never was really a numbers guy.

"When Daniel was working in Roseville, he worked 10-14 hours a week. What do you think, Daniel? Would you like to work that many hours, or maybe a few more?" I asked, prompting him.

"Yes," Daniel wisely answered, picking up on my cue. But it was too late.

"I'm sorry," the manager replied, "but with our hiring fair, we just don't have any openings right now. I'll put your resume on file, Daniel, and keep you in mind for any openings we might have in the future." We never heard from him again.

From being a shoo-in to being shooed out the door, Lunds and Byerly's was a complete flop. Strike three. We knew when

SPECIAL

we were defeated and yielded to the experts, calling Kourtney Wright, our Vocational Rehabilitation contact.

Meeting with Kourtney was a triumphant return for Daniel. He had worked with her in high school. Familiarity bred an easy banter back and forth between them at our onboarding meeting. Kourtney, in fact, had been one of those instrumental in making Bethel a reality for us. Now we turned to her again, hoping she could resurrect some of her magic.

After listening to our plight, she provided us with three options for career counseling and support. We questioned her extensively on each of the options and landed on our choice: Lindsey, a specialist in job placement and early support. Within a couple weeks, Lindsey was meeting with us to create a job profile for Daniel. In creating a list of must-haves for a prospective job, we collectively came up with two. First, Daniel needed a job that offered regular interactions with a consistent populace. Second, he'd benefit from a job with repetitive tasks. We felt that under these two working conditions, Daniel would thrive. Lindsey was then tasked with assessing Daniel's strengths and desires. What emerged from all of this was a Top Jobs list they planned to attack together: from applying, to interviewing, to hopefully accepting an offer.

Limited by location, tops on Daniel's wish list was Target, followed by working food service for the Farmington schools. He and Lindsey began meeting weekly at libraries or coffee shops to search job listings and submit applications. We finally felt as if we were gaining traction, even as summer was beginning to wind down. But then the Lord threw us a curveball.

In this time of transition, our new case manager, Chris, really pressed us to consider drafting a Person Centered Plan for

JOY CLINE

Daniel. A Person Centered Plan helps those with disabilities articulate their wishes and dreams, and map out a plan for their future. Lacking direction at this point, we bought into it. Chris recommended Mark Winters of Owakihi, Inc., and scheduled a meeting with him.

Some people come into your life, and you feel as though you have known them for forever. Mark was one of those people. Mark began by explaining that "Owakihi" was the Lakota word for "I am able." It was his hope that Daniel would exact a sense of control over his future in the voicing of his dreams. Further, it was his hope that Daniel would be enabled to turn these dreams into reality. Mark's role was to coax those wishes and dreams out of Daniel through a series of probing questions. The afternoon he came to our home, he took copious notes, disarming Daniel with his humor and stories. Mark also talked to Geoff and me, all the while piecing together a pretty spot-on profile of Daniel. When the dust had settled from an afternoon with Mark, we had a date on our calendars, August 1st, for the unveiling of Daniel's plan.

This plan was a big deal. As such, Mark encouraged us to make it momentous for Daniel. We planned a special dinner and invited all the family, including Gramps. By now Gramps was becoming more and more immobile. It took both Geoff and Ben to hoist him up our back steps and into a waiting chair in our family room. It would be the last time he was able to visit our home. We also invited Chris and Kourtney. As those from the county who were working directly with Daniel, we knew we would benefit from their expertise to help put Daniel's plans into motion.

Mark set up the room with a large piece of paper taped to the wall. Daniel was given the chair of honor up front next to Mark. He didn't necessarily enjoy being the center of all this attention. Prone to clam up in such circumstances, Daniel was kept talking by his rapport with Mark and the prompts that kept coming at him. As Daniel responded, Mark summarized his words on the large piece of paper. With markers and chalk in hand, he mapped out Daniel's dreams in words and illustrations. Before long, one page grew into two, until both were filled with a beautiful future.

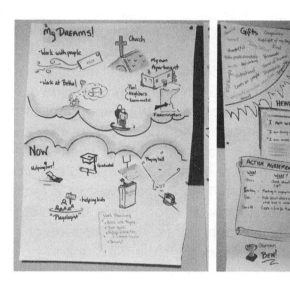

While not entirely surprised by the dreams taking shape on the paper, two of Daniel's responses caught me off guard. When Mark asked Daniel whether he saw himself getting married, he said, "Yes." And Mark went on to draw a husband and wife. I was left to wonder what had changed since receiving David's distraught text from just a few months earlier: "Hi this is David kaetterhenry here in our class he dose not want kids and he said he is not getting a wife what should I do to help him." Apparently, Daniel no longer needed David's help in that area. Second, when asked about his dream job, he hesitated. Allison countered his silence with a question of her own. "You loved your time at Bethel, what would you think about working there?" New to the family as having been married to Ben

JOY CLINE

just under a year, Allison's words carried more weight than all the rest of the family's combined. Pleaser Daniel nodded his head vigorously to Allison's suggestion. And so it was written down for posterity that Daniel's dream job would be to work at Bethel. Although I think *anything* Allison would have suggested would have been met with a vigorous head-shaking affirmation, it just so happened it was Bethel that became the "dream job" that day. Her question was Holy Spirit inspired indeed.

Mark then turned to the larger group for input into Daniel's gifts. We all joined in with a chorus of affirming qualities we saw in Daniel: kind, compassionate, thoughtful, dependable, honest, intentional, having a sense of humor, and a lover of people. He sat a little taller in his chair in the glow of such praise from those who know him best. Mark also turned to the group to identify "roadblocks" in making Daniel's wishes a reality. An ongoing one was, of course, transportation. But a surprising one recognized Daniel's penchant to "wait for someone else" to take action for him. Mark wisely added action points to counter the roadblocks and ensure these dreams weren't left to fester on paper. Tasked with seeing these action points to completion was Ben, who had volunteered to be Daniel's "champion."

Ben proved to be the perfect man for the job. For hardly a week had gone by, and he was in heavy pursuit of securing employment for Daniel.

"Have you reached out to Bethel yet?" He asked.

I had to admit we hadn't. Geoff and I *had* talked about it though, and determined Daniel's best hope for employment at Bethel would probably be through its food service, Sodexo. Daniel thought so too. He loved food and was one of the Dining

SPECIAL

Center's most faithful customers. In fact, so akin was he to the Dining Center and its staff that at Daniel's graduation, Geoff took the opportunity to thank the employees for all the ways they had served Daniel throughout his time at Bethel. On hand that night was Bob Schuchardt, Sodexo's general manager. He was quick to retort: "I love Daniel! If he ever wants a job, I'd hire him in a New York minute!"

Recalling Bob's words, I hit the online campus job listings. But a quick perusal of openings at Sodexo revealed only a dishwashing position, decidedly a back-room job. Daniel was an out-front kind of guy. Were we settling, just to make this happen? I had my reservations. Add to this that Bethel was still a fifty-minute drive across the Twin Cities metro. The transportation piece remained a roadblock of seismic proportions. I clicked out of the Sodexo job openings.

But Ben would not let us off the hook that easily. He encouraged us to apply. His insistence caught me off guard. It was easy for the "champion" to call the shots from his armchair position. It was quite another thing to be the ones who had to make it happen on a daily basis. I challenged him right back. "How can we apply for a job we have no way of getting Daniel to? Shouldn't we figure that out first?" Then for good measure, I added, "It's unsustainable, and I'd hate to burn any bridges."

"Just apply," he responded with certainty.

One of my all-time favorite movie scenes is from the Indiana Jones film, *The Last Crusade.* In it, Indy is asked to take a leap of faith…literally. At cliff's edge and faced with a wide and deep chasm, he is bid to cross in order to save the life of a friend on the other side. Indy hesitates momentarily in the impossibility of it all, but then steps off into sheer nothingness…only to be upheld by unseen forces.

JOY CLINE

Ben's request left us at cliff's edge, stymied by our own faithlessness. Yet at Ben's urging, Geoff crafted an email to Bob over the weekend. We hemmed and hawed before finally clicking the send button...our own puny leap of faith into the great unknown. That click felt decidedly like a step off the cliff to us, a point of no return. We were either all in, or we were making a huge mistake we couldn't sustain. We were certain to find out if Bob *really* meant he'd hire Daniel "in a New York minute."

Unknown to us at that time, Dawn had simultaneously messaged all the recent BUILD graduates that weekend with a job opportunity: working the pasta line in the Dining Center at Bethel. Daniel had seen Dawn's message, and hadn't said a word...to Dawn or to us. When a chance encounter revealed to me the missed job opportunity, I was furious with Daniel at his indifference and lackadaisical response. Here was the very job we had been praying for...an out-front sort of job, his "dream job" at Bethel. Yet Daniel was stymied—"waiting for someone else"—the very roadblock we had been warned of in our meeting with Mark.

I marched Daniel up to his bedroom where the two posters from his Person Centered Plan draped his bulletin board for inspiration. As we reviewed it together, we had a "Come to Jesus" moment about whether the truth on these posters was really the truth written across his heart. And if so, what needed to change. Within minutes, Daniel was responding to Dawn's message, saying he "was interested" in the pasta line job.

And then, we waited...for Bob, for Dawn, for a job. Meanwhile, we carried on with the everyday, the commonplace, and prayed for God to move us in the right direction with Daniel. The everyday for us meant walking Lizzy, our Border Collie.

SPECIAL

If we didn't, she would most certainly remind us. But this Sunday morning walk would be different.

As Geoff and I walked the neighborhood that morning—the same neighborhood we walked twice a day, day after day, year after year—inspiration struck. Passing the house two doors down from us, I saw the home of the Heikkilas. Their home looked much the same...yellow house with burgundy trim, lots of cars in the driveway. Years back, when the house had gone up for sale, we faithfully prayed together as a family that the Lord would bring us new neighbors who were Christians. The Heikkilas were the embodiment of those prayers. Over the years we would join together with them for a neighborhood Bible study and in planning the annual neighborhood picnic. Mary would even babysit their two boys, Isaac and Micah, from time to time...her first babysitting job. But this day, my mind was elsewhere, and the Lord seized on my desperation.

Recognizing the cars in the driveway, I thought of the boys. Isaac and Micah must be home. Isaac was a college senior at the University of Northwestern—St. Paul. Micah would be joining him there in a matter of weeks as a high school senior taking on-campus PSEO classes. Rather than living on campus, the two chose to make the long, arduous, forty-five minute commute to school each day.

Wait! The long, arduous, forty-five minute commute each day? That same long, arduous forty-five minute commute was just an additional five-minute drive from Bethel. Would they? Could they? I shared my inspiration with Geoff, who immediately called Doug, the boys' dad, and left a message. Meanwhile, we worked out the details to our pitch on the remainder of our walk.

JOY CLINE

But a pitch was hardly needed. When we threw out the possibility of Daniel getting a job at Bethel and needing a ride each weekday, Doug passed it on to Isaac who didn't even blink. Sure, he'd take Daniel, if all their schedules aligned. It would be a crowded ride with backpacks in tow in their little silver Toyota Prius hybrid, but the cost for gas would be minimal, split three ways.

Geoff and I marveled at how God was pulling this all together. But isn't that the way He works? If I will just muster enough faith to step out—without having everything already figured out—isn't that when I often see some of His best work? In our leap of faith, we were upheld by unseen forces. But ours had a name to them...God. In knocking down the monstrosity of the transportation roadblock, it seemed a mere formality for God to provide the job as well.

The next day, Bob called us, and he was as good as his word. He offered Daniel the job as the new pasta line worker for Sodexo at Bethel without even an interview. With the school year bearing down, he wondered, could Daniel come the next morning for training? He most certainly could, and I would have him there at 8:00 sharp!

The early morning drive to Bethel that next day was anticlimactic. Even as we awaited the details of the job itself, it already bore the handprints of God all over it. I just knew He would take care of the rest. As if to scoff at our puny plans, en route to Bethel Daniel received calls from both Target and Farmington Schools, offering him an interview for openings they had. He told them, "Thanks, but I already have a job." And I heard him do so with an inflection of pride to his voice.

Daniel's role, we were to find that day, would be as an assistant to Ulysses on the made-to-order pasta line. It would be his job to dish up the customer's vegetable choices, wash the sauté pans used for each order, and refill any vegetables running low. It was a job that kept him hopping with hardly a dull moment. Add to that the unlimited opportunities for interactions in a long line of students and staff at Bethel, and it hardly felt like a job to Daniel! He came home filled to the brim.

Of course, the last hurdle in all this was whether Daniel's schedule would mesh with Isaac and Micah's. Daniel was to work Monday through Friday from 10:45-2:30, the busy lunch shift. The boys had to be there decidedly earlier and, at times, stay later—hardly an inconvenience for Daniel! He just resorted back to his best Bethel days in making his daily rounds to the BUILD office, Admissions, the Office of Christian Formation, and generally to anyone who had two minutes to spare for a conversation. A few extra hours at Bethel were not a hardship for him! And…he was able to attend Chapel again. Of course, unlike his days as a student, he had to slip out twenty minutes early in order to make it to work on time. But he *did* make it to pre-Chapel prayer! It was a pretty sweet gig!

As wonderful as the job appeared, it was not without its obstacles. Over time, they emerged and temporarily knocked us off kilter. I got used to finding the gaps between the schedules of the two different universities. Gaps meant I was Daniel's fill-in driver. I tried to anticipate them so I could block myself from teaching those days. Another obstacle was that Isaac ended up graduating at mid term. You can bet the Clines were praying in earnest for Micah to pass his driver's test in December so he could assume driving duties in January. He did, but the prayers didn't end there. Just as earnestly, we prayed for Micah and Daniel's safe commutes, particularly on those treacherous Minnesota snow days. It was a whole other level of trust to release Daniel to the passenger seat of a relatively inexperienced driver in a pipsqueak of a car.

And then there was Covid. Daniel was still in his first year of working for Sodexo when it hit…abruptly. When he left work that Friday, March 13, 2020, in high spirits for his spring break, he had no idea it would be the last day he would work that year. None of us did. Thus began those dark months of nothingness that we tried as a family to provide shape to by designating game nights, movie nights, and bonfire nights—anything to help us keep track of the days of the week as they slipped steadily by us in chaotic formlessness.

Fortunately, by the time fall rolled around, colleges had reimagined themselves and were now offering a hybrid style of learning that was both distant and limited in-person. As college students began to once again emerge on campus, Daniel returned to work as well, albeit with a face mask and a new title—"essential worker."

And while nothing had changed, everything had changed. Daniel still worked the pasta line on campus, but gone was the made-to-order option. What remained was a pre-made version of pasta that Daniel merely dished up for students. Both the job and the student experience had been diminished immeasurably. Add to that the limited interactions, as masks shielded smiles from both server and the served. The

SPECIAL

job certainly lost its sheen for a season, but all jobs had. Daniel merely soldiered on.

Another prominent change facing us that fall of 2020, was the loss of the Heikkila Brothers Express to get Daniel to Bethel every day. Isaac had graduated and was now employed, and Micah had chosen to attend college in Texas. While in another season of life this loss might have been more pronounced, the answer to this Covid season transportation roadblock was simple: me. Though public schools in the area had resumed classes in a limited capacity, it was nothing I desired to step into as a substitute teacher. Instead, I became Daniel's ride to Bethel for the 2020-21 school year, while taking some online teaching relicensure classes. Fortunately, Geoff spared me the drive one day a week, conducting his weekly flexible learning day from Bethel.

With time, Daniel adapted to doing his job differently. We all did, though I think it especially significant for a young man with autism. And despite the curveballs thrown at him, Daniel continued to bloom where he was planted—no matter the ever-changing landscape. As a result, the impact that began as a student at Bethel continued as a Dining Center worker at Bethel.

As Daniel's designated chauffeur, I was given a little glimpse into this impact each day I accompanied him on campus. Greetings of "Hi Daniel!" cascaded down the hall. Hardly ever did we meet with a silent walk, masks or no masks.

Somehow, it never took long for Daniel to attain first-name status with others. One Labor Day weekend in church during the call to greet those around us, we turned around to shake hands with a young man who was new to us. As we did, a smile broke across his face."Wait!" He exclaimed, eying up Daniel, "I know you! You work at Bethel! It's Daniel, right?"

Josh was his name, and we were to learn he was a freshman at Bethel who had been in school a mere five days. Yet Daniel was one of the connections he had made. We marveled at the recognition for such a short span of time. Josh obviously liked his pasta!

Short or long. Big or small. Daniel was making his mark at Bethel one interaction at a time. When I think back to his first birthday while a student at Bethel, I feared it would pass unrecognized. Now I know his birthdays will be a chorus of affirmation not orchestrated by me. Others, such as Annie Allen, wife of current Bethel President Ross Allen, will make sure the day is heralded. Annie has taken up the charge to celebrate Daniel every September 19th. Whether leading the Dining Center in a rousing rendition of "Happy Birthday to You" or fashioning a birthday crown for his head, she has elevated him and made sure he is seen. And, of course, the BUILD staff never forget to mark his special day with their affirmations, a card, and a Royal Grounds drink. As a mom, such gestures fill me with gratitude.

But beyond gratitude, Daniel's work at Bethel has given me moments to ponder and treasure, of the Mary sort in Luke 2:19, as she bore witness to her Son Jesus' influence.[20] One such moment came at a Chapel service in a series entitled "God @Work." In his sermon, Nate Gustafson, Associate Dean for Campus Engagement at Bethel, was attempting to drive home the point to students to view all their work as a form of worship to God.

---

[20] *Bible gateway passage: Luke 2:19 - new international version.* Bible Gateway. (n.d.-e). https://www.biblegateway.com/passage/?search=Luke+2%3A19&version=NIV

SPECIAL

"You know, somebody who embodies this on campus is Daniel Cline, who works in food service," Nate said. "I can't tell you how many days I feel seen and I feel loved. Because when I walk in, he's always saying 'hello' to me. It doesn't matter if I'm across the room or right next to him. He does his job with excellence, and he does it with love."[21]

Work has become so much more to Daniel than just a job. It's another way he worships God, and he does it well.

---

[21] YouTube. (n.d.). YouTube. https://www.youtube.com/watch?v=0XqLbN5qOPk

19

THANKFUL FOR THIN WALLS

Daniel's work became an outlet for his worship, and he did some of his best work during Covid despite its restrictions and limitations. While his smile was hidden, somehow his joy remained maskless. During the 2020-21 school year, I beheld this joy as we made the long commute to and from Bethel each day. His chatter was a welcome addition to the bleak landscape and endless miles.

"We're at a marginal risk for severe weather today."

"We ran out of pasta at lunch."

"Who do you think is preaching this weekend?"

"The Vikings are missing a linebacker and a receiver for Sunday."

"There's a new billboard!"

A steady stream bombarded me—a random collection of his day—with our 70's playlist bridging any brief gaps. And while I delighted in this sweet season with Daniel, I also knew in the back of my mind that it was just that, a season, and one that was unsustainable for the long term.

SPECIAL

In Sodexo, Daniel now had a job that offered him a measure of security. Even though Covid had dismantled the food industry, he remained employed, and that gave us reason to hope. To be sure, we were still fully entrenched in a global pandemic as we began the New Year of 2021, yet we allowed ourselves to peer further down the page of Daniel's Person Centered Plan to that other facet of his independence: securing housing.

Looking to launch your child towards independent living is one thing, but looking to launch your child during a global pandemic is an entirely different thing. Yet time was at my disposal as I played chauffeur for Daniel. I decided to use some of this free time to research available housing options.

In considering housing for Daniel, I focused on many of the traditional options. Daniel's good buddy, Jake, lived on his own in an apartment supported by a company's community coordinators, who checked in on him and provided activities. While this seemed a great fit for Jake, we knew Daniel's endless stream of conversation begged for a roommate. Disability providers, such as Jake uses, prefer clients living on their own in order to better coordinate individual services.

Another option was the AbleLight Village, a community that combines housing for those fifty-five and older with those of intellectual and developmental disabilities. It offers a layer of oversight in the community sense, while providing activities and classes for residents. The problem with AbleLight Village for us was its location. It was a fifty-five minute drive from home and a similar commute to his work at Bethel. Still, we were intrigued enough to begin attending mobilization meetings for a potential spin-off housing community much closer to Bethel. Unfortunately, despite already having purchased land, the development fell through.

JOY CLINE

Hammer Residences were at the intersection of both Jake's serviced apartment and AbleLight Village. Clients live in their own individual apartment in a section of a larger apartment complex reserved exclusively for Hammer clients. So while clients receive individual care, they also benefit from the community sense of living together, much like the dorms at Bethel. Like the other two options, they also offer activities. But unlike the others, they provide a communal dinner each night. This really appealed to us—especially considering Daniel's limitations in preparing meals of substance, variety, and nutritional balance. And as much as Daniel loves his food, he also loves people. However, once again the transportation roadblock rose up to topple our hopes. Hammer's apartments were exclusive to the west Twin Cities metro, a surmountable distance from Bethel.

A relatively new option at the time was an organization called Rumi, which connects people having a disability with a compatible, supportive roommate. Rumi roommates work together to secure their own housing. It was a simple concept, but could it work? A couple of girls from the cohort after Daniel's had tried Rumi for a few months with limited success. The selling point in this housing option, of course, was having a companion there most of the time...but only if it was the *right* companion. A living situation could quickly become quite sour with the wrong one.

Never really on our radar for Daniel were group homes. Geoff had spent a couple of summers painting for some—enough time to decide it probably wasn't the best option for our son. Besides, Minnesota was slowly shifting from group homes as the end-all in disability housing.

Beyond these traditional options, we also gleaned from the experience of Owakihi's Mark Winters. In his parting meeting

SPECIAL

with us, Mark supplied us with abundant resources for both employment and housing. I was particularly struck by his housing ideas, as many were ones that pieced together housing and services. I had never even thought possible most of the ideas he presented to us. He expanded my limited preconceptions of Daniel's options.

As I weighed the pluses and minuses of all these housing options from my Covid hangout perch near the rafters of Bethel's Benson Great Hall, I grew increasingly overwhelmed. To recenter my focus, I turned once again to Daniel's Person Centered Plan. When asked to describe his dream place, Daniel had stated he wanted a home with a pool, neighbors, and a roommate. Summing these wishes up, Mark had drawn an apartment building and entitled it "Daniel's apartment." When further pressed on where he wanted to live, Daniel responded, "Farmington." But then he did something very un-Daniel-like, adding, "...in a house." As one who is content to mostly follow along with the wishes of others and let matters lie, Daniel's insistent desire for a house met my ears as a shout. At that moment, I remember thinking, *"That's* never going to happen!" I couldn't envision him ever having the means by which a house would be an option as a living situation. And if I was being honest, the pool seemed a bit of a stretch as well, though his friend Jake's apartment had one.

Now over a year later, even his wish to live in Farmington seemed unattainable with his job at Bethel now driving our search. The confluence of Daniel's dreams for a home and his actual housing options simply weren't coming together. Geoff and I, of course, prayed together for this new living situation for Daniel. It had been one of our long-standing prayers in life, as we wanted to avoid saddling Mary or Ben with the full responsibility of taking on Daniel one day in our absence. I think this is a prayer of nearly all parents of special needs

JOY CLINE

children. But in making the daily drive to Bethel, it was taking on a whole new urgency for me.

"I think you should talk to Dawn," Geoff suggested.

"She's too busy," was my quick retort. Bethel had just started the new semester, and I knew it was a heavy-handed time in the BUILD office accustoming students to their new schedules. Besides, Daniel was no longer in the program. Dawn had enough on her plate without troubling her with the needs of a former student.

"I think she could bring a lot of clarity to this for us."

Geoff was right that in Dawn, I had one of the best experts under roof. And in being at Bethel four days a week, I certainly had the flexibility of schedule to meet a gap in hers. Still, I dug my heels in, too proud, somehow, to bother her and ask for help. Instead, I plowed forward with my Google searches. But even as I did, the Lord began nudging me to submit to my husband's request, that pride was not something to harbor. I knew His Word had something to say about both submission and pride. Reluctantly, I submitted and texted Dawn, "Hey, any chance you'd have some time for a chat? I'd love to get your mind on something." Then to appease my guilt, I added, "How about I bring you lunch?" Click. Send. My small step of obedience.

Despite my skewed ideas otherwise, Dawn prioritized time for me in her schedule. So within a week, here I was, Chipotle in hand, knocking on her door. She invited me into her office where we spread out our pandemic carry-out meal as if it were a feast. Despite campus mandates, I was thankful for the time our lunch afforded us to connect without masks.

SPECIAL

As is often the case with Dawn, we touched on many fronts before landing on the questions foremost on my mind. I had carefully rehearsed them in my head, hoping to capitalize on this opportunity. My questions were really twofold: I wanted to know which housing option she had found most successful for former BUILD students and which she saw as the best fit for Daniel. I knew she was uniquely positioned to provide me with valued insights into both. Dawn didn't disappoint. She told me the things she liked about some of the housing choices BUILD graduates had made. We also talked about the limitations of those choices. Ultimately, she believed Daniel would most succeed in a setting with a roommate and with opportunities to gather socially. She knew Daniel well. He loves his people. It was the reason he voiced in his Person Centered Plan that he wanted to live with a roommate and neighbors. With that in mind, together we began exploring potential roommates for him from amongst recent BUILD graduates.

Dawn also sent me out the door with some resources: a pamphlet and a magnet with the website for Minnesota housing benefits, mn.hb101.org.[22] The latter proved extremely helpful. In creating an account for Daniel, I was able to access a search engine that explored how much Daniel could afford to pay for housing while providing resources he might tap into to help pay for it.

While it wasn't earth shattering, the meeting with Dawn crystallized my scattered thoughts and redirected me back to what was foundational in Daniel's housing search—people. I left with a lot to think about and plenty to share with Geoff. The next morning as I sat in my Covid perch at Bethel, my plans were reinvigorated and had a direction again. But that's when I should have stopped and taken note…they were "my plans."

---

[22] HB101 Minnesota - Home. (n.d.). https://mn.hb101.org/

JOY CLINE

Proverbs 19:21 reads: "Many are the plans in a person's heart, but it is the Lord's purpose that prevails."[23]

As a planner, this Scripture has tormented me through the years. For in it, I must always succumb to the puniness of all my own plans before my all-knowing Sovereign Lord, whose ways are *always* higher and better. This time was to be no exception.

Even as I sat in the midst of my planning, a text interrupted me. It was Dawn. "Thank you for such a lovely lunch yesterday! I absolutely loved learning more about you and your journey, and all you are considering as part of Daniel's journey. God is at work to meet you in this exploration, and you will see that more when you get an email from Ryan today."

My mind raced with her words…"God is at work to meet you in this exploration…" What did she mean? I checked my inbox. Nothing. But I kept checking until a message finally appeared from Ryan Anderson, BUILD's Jobs and Employment professor and Internship Supervisor.

Ryan was a fixture in the BUILD office. He had been with the team in one capacity or another since Daniel's freshman year at Bethel. Besides teaching job skills to the BUILD students, it was Ryan's job to coordinate and oversee the students' internships. This included training and supervising the job mentors, traditional Bethel students who accompanied the BUILD students to their jobs to help them out.

Ryan's email got right to the point. He had been in the office yesterday and happened to overhear my conversation with

---

[23] *Bible gateway passage: Proverbs 19:21 - new international version*. Bible Gateway. (n.d.-i). https://www.biblegateway.com/passage/?search=Proverbs+19%3A21&version=NIV

SPECIAL

Dawn about housing options. The walls can be quite thin at Bethel. A couple of hours later, Bethel student, Logan Fisco, walked into his office. Logan had been Daniel's job mentor when he worked as a Playologist at the Children's Museum in St. Paul. Every Saturday morning the two of them would load up the van and head to St. Paul. They had a blast together playing with the kids at the museums' exhibits, sometimes celebrating over lunch on the way back to Bethel. Logan was a great guy. Three years later, Logan was now a senior. He still helped out as a job mentor, but was nearing his graduation and planning on enrolling in Bethel's Seminary in the fall. His mind was on just that as he entered Ryan's office that day. Logan had heard about Rumi, the organization that pairs a disabled individual with a roommate, and wanted to learn more about it. As he looked out on his future, he thought Rumi just might enable him to stick close to Bethel, attend classes, help someone out, and pay down some of his college debt. He just had to find the right person.

Ryan took in all Logan was saying to him, amazed at the timing. He gave Logan what he knew about Rumi, but then divulged his overheard conversation from earlier that day. He recognized this was more than mere coincidence.

"What?! Really?!" Logan's eyes alighted. "I just had lunch with Daniel a couple of weeks ago!" He saw the God moment for what it was as well.

Ryan closed his email to me by asking if he could send my contact information to Logan to begin a conversation about a possible Rumi relationship with Daniel. I couldn't type the word, "Absolutely!" quick enough.

Within a couple of days, Logan reached out to me. In the meantime, I had done my homework on Rumi. I learned that

JOY CLINE

Daniel was going to need a DD Waiver in order to fund any support, that same DD waiver that had eluded him when we tried to apply before Bethel.

It seemed Logan had done his research as well. He asked great questions, particularly in regards to Daniel's needed level of care. For our part, Geoff and I tried to identify all the ways we stepped in to help Daniel across his day. We wanted to ensure Logan knew what he was signing up for, as best we could. But could we ever condense a lifetime of caring for Daniel into a single conversation? It certainly helped that Logan already knew Daniel and was aware of some of his limitations from having served as his job mentor.

In the end, we left the conversation with both of us taking a step back to pray over it. Logan wanted to check in with his parents, as well as some guys he had already committed to move in with after graduation. And we, of course, had to talk to Daniel— a formidable task indeed. For how far along we already were into this process, we still hadn't brought this housing opportunity up to him yet. I think in the back of our minds, Geoff and I wanted to make sure it truly had legs before surfacing the battle that would surely ensue. We recalled the fist fight it was to get him out of his comfort zone and into Bethel. This loomed as an even larger battle in our minds. It meant not living with "Mom, Dad, and Lizzy...FOREVER!" And, unlike Bethel, it had no graduation end date. Yet there was enough in Logan's thoughts, his mature approach, and in his track record of maintaining relationship with Daniel over the years to believe "God was at work to meet us in this exploration," just as Dawn had foretold. We just needed to enter into the fray with Daniel. We decided Sunday afternoon would be the best. As with the Bethel decision, we assembled our best prayer warriors to go before us in preparing Daniel's heart with their prayers.

SPECIAL

We knew we were about to rock his world. While Daniel knew moving out on his own was always the end game, he didn't see it coming now. There is a huge difference from having something out there in the distant future to having it dumped in your lap. As such, we treaded lightly, taking the angle that it was Logan who was seeking out a possible Rumi relationship with *him*. It's nice to feel wanted. We reassured him he could still come home some weekends to see Lizzy, go to church with us, and have movie nights.

But for all our anticipation to the contrary, our conversation with Daniel went remarkably well. He didn't argue, He didn't bristle. He didn't seem overly anxious. He didn't even ask those follow-up questions that betray the churning going on in his mind. God had most certainly prepared his heart.

I guess it was as Dawn said…it all comes down to people for Daniel. And in the embodiment of Logan, God had chosen the right person with whom Daniel felt a measure of comfort—enough comfort, in fact, to even be willing to move away from home.

A couple of weeks later, we weren't surprised when Logan acquiescenced to this Rumi relationship. He wondered if we could make the move-in date for May 1st. May 1st, however, was just two months away. We had a lot to do to meet that deadline. Foremost, we had to secure a DD waiver for Daniel from the county. Without it, the dream opportunity was over. We were assured, however, that this was a mere formality. County representatives said when Daniel was ready to move out, they'd be able to get him the waiver. But could they do it fast—like two months fast?

By now we had yet another case manager, Nicole, who was relatively young and inexperienced, but who made up for it in

JOY CLINE

her energy level. We tasked her with helping us to the finish line. There were several steps to securing the waiver. First, Daniel had to have a fresh MN Choice Assessment done to determine his level of care. Then, he needed approval from a county committee simply to *petition* for the waiver. Finally, and most importantly, he needed authorization for the DD waiver itself. It was a daunting process made all the more insurmountable because of Covid and a tight timeline. MN Choice Assessments, we were told, were currently running months behind. But Nicole assured us she would do her best to stress the urgency of Daniel's situation and hopefully get him bumped up in line. She brought in her supervisor at Thomas Allen Inc., and the two of them went at it hard.

Meanwhile, under assurances it was only a matter of time until we worked through these processes, we moved forward as well, inviting Logan down to our house for dinner to work through some details. If Geoff and I had any doubts in pursuing this Rumi relationship, Logan certainly laid them to rest that night. His genuineness was clearly evident in his soft-spoken interactions with Daniel. He leveled with him as a friend, coaxing responses of more than just one word out of him. As we sought common ground in our vision for this relationship, Logan deferred to Daniel, making sure his wishes were heard. That was huge for us.

One of those wishes was for a house. While I was thinking about an apartment all the way, Logan came alongside Daniel.

"What do you think, Daniel? Should we live in a house?" Logan asked enthusiastically. "We can mow the lawn and shovel the walks together!"

While I thought his enthusiasm for yard work was a little misplaced, Daniel did not. He matched Logan's enthusiasm.

SPECIAL

"Yes!" He responded. "I'd like to mow and shovel with you, Logan!"

Clearly they were in the infatuation stage of house living. I was certain it would only be a matter of time before these same household chores would lose their luster. Yet I didn't want to rain on their parade, even if I still had my doubts whether a house could even be feasible under the mutual budget we had set.

In all this planning, Geoff and I had only one request. We asked whatever home they chose to be within a two-mile radius of Bethel. Transportation still posed a major roadblock for Daniel. Two miles gave him the option of walking or riding his bike to work, making him dependent upon no one but himself.

Drawing a two-mile concentric circle around Bethel, we began our search. We were looking for a two bedroom place within our budget and with a lease starting in May, a tall task indeed in a market driven by college students mostly still under lease for the school year. While I hit my Google search that exclusively surfaced apartments, Logan had an entirely different approach, scouring social media. In the end, it was Logan who found a place first on Facebook Marketplace.

"Hey, I think I found one. It's a house in New Brighton…704 Tenth St. NW, the upper unit. But we need to act fast. Any chance you can meet me there at 11:00?"

A house! Really? Could it be? Was God meeting Daniel and his voiced desire once again? It seemed too good to be true; but then again, we serve a mighty God!

We changed our Saturday morning plans and rushed to New Brighton, where we met Logan and his dad in the driveway.

JOY CLINE

The house wasn't much of a looker from the outside. While quite large, it appeared a little tired in its two-toned brown paint with overgrown landscaping, gravel driveway, and a rickety deck. Together we climbed the deck steps holding on to the railing for added support. There was yet another stairway that led to the unit itself. If the outside looked bad, this stairway was downright creepy. It was tight, steep, creaky, and dusty with cobwebs and dead bugs galore! Maybe this was what affordability looked like for a house rental in the area. The mom in me cringed, but I tried to keep an open mind as we entered the unit.

The upstairs itself was decidedly better. It was incredibly spacious, featuring ten-foot ceilings and plenty of large windows that flooded the space with light. It had a kitchen with loads of cupboards and counter space, and room enough for an eat-in table and chairs. There was even a separate dining room as well. Its ceilings sloped and arched in ways that were decidedly cozy. The place was growing on us.

As we surveyed it, trying to take it all in, we spied other suitors waiting in the driveway for their chance to nab the rental. We knew we didn't have the luxury to sit on this decision. It was gut check time. Huddling together, Logan, his dad, Geoff, Daniel, and I found we were all on the same page. We told Dan, the landlord, that we were in and negotiated a start date for the beginning of May. The boys signed a year-long lease, which we co-signed for Daniel. This was now officially Daniel's home for at least the next year. Though he was quick to add, "I have TWO homes!" He wasn't quite ready to jump all in.

Coming under contract unleashed a whole new level of searching to furnish it. Following Logan's lead, I caught on quickly and became a pro at Facebook Marketplace. Of course, it didn't hurt that my chauffeur duties afforded me

SPECIAL

the dedicated time to master it. As I found what I thought were treasures or steals, I shared pictures with Daniel and Logan before purchasing. Logan had a clear style and vision for the place, while Daniel liked everything. A Google doc helped to minimize duplicates as both families rushed to secure the necessary items. Soon our house became cluttered with the stuff of another household: a couch, kitchen table, dining room table, chairs, bed, dresser, microwave cart, microwave, lamps, vacuum cleaner, steam mop, pots, pans, plates, utensils...the list went on and on. My house grew smaller and smaller in their temporary storage.

By now we had jumped through all the hoops with the county. Nicole had managed to expedite Daniel's case, though I'm sure God was in the details. And now, Logan and Daniel were officially roommates-to-be! Rumi staff scheduled an intake meeting with us all to establish expectations and set goals for Daniel's growth. It involved a lot of input from both boys, though we found ourselves having to jump in from time to time to clarify and expound on Daniel's wishes. The final decision needed no help from us at all: What would they like for a housewarming gift? Logan looked at Daniel, and Daniel looked at Logan; together they chimed, "A Target gift card!"

Amidst the flurry of the final weeks before move-in day, an unwelcome visitor made a reappearance out of nowhere. One moment we were watching television together, the next Daniel was looking at me funny, as if trying to focus, color draining from his face. I knew the look. I dashed upstairs and grabbed a bowl, but by the time I reached him he was already retching. Though it had been fourteen years since the last chance meeting, his unexplained sickness was back. It roiled him until I had to admit defeat in my own attempts to subdue it. I brought him to our local clinic, before they forwarded us to the hospital emergency room.

JOY CLINE

It was April of 2021, and Covid procedures were still in place, which meant masks and limited visitation. Poor Daniel! Sick as a dog, and he could hardly breathe through the mask! To make matters worse, when they collected him to bring him back for testing, they stopped me at the door and said, "I'm sorry, but you're not allowed to go with him."

As Daniel disappeared through the hospital doors, his wide eyes scared and pleading with me, my fierce mother instincts took over. "What do you mean, I can't go back there?" I protested. "He's a mentally disabled young adult. He's vulnerable!"

"I'm sorry, Miss. You can take a chair over there." As I sat down stewing and firing off texts for prayer, it wasn't long before calmer heads prevailed. A nurse opened the door, calling out, "Mother of Daniel Cline?" I jumped to my feet, ready to double back on my protests. But this time, she was inviting me to join Daniel in the back. I dashed to his side, squeezing his hand and reassuring him I would stay with him.

Once again, the doctor ran Daniel through a battery of tests, most of them the same as from our last ER visit, though this time I didn't have Geoff or Kristin for support. The wait in the emergency room is always excruciating—watching your loved one suffer while they attempt to determine the cause. All the while, you are trying to mask your fears, praying and hoping they will soon administer something—anything—that will bring a measure of relief.

Our wait was long, but the results were immediate. As the fluids and meds finally found their spot, Daniel began talking a little more...always a good sign. His headache and dizziness subsided. His eyes regained their sparkle. By the time the doctor emerged with the test results, I felt like I already had my boy back. The findings revealed nothing alarming, though a few

SPECIAL

numbers were a little off. I thanked God. The emergency room doctor recommended we connect with our primary physician in the coming days for a follow-up. The doctor turned to leave, but my biggest question hadn't been answered: Why?

"Why is this happening to Daniel?" I blurted out, drawing him back in the room. "What's causing this?"

The doctor admitted he was stumped, but reassured me that I could bring Daniel back if it ever resurfaced again. I wasn't satisfied. What *was* this mysterious illness that returned to upend Daniel's life and twist me up inside just as we were about to launch him? The timing jarred me. After *all* we had seen God do to get us to this point, I began to question everything. Were we doing the right thing in placing Daniel under the care and supervision of Logan? Logan was even younger than Daniel in age! Would he recognize the onset of Daniel's illness if it were to resurface? Could Logan care for him until we made our way across the Twin Cities? Overnight, the distance became an issue all over again. And as with Bethel, the core issue came down to trust. Could I entrust Daniel into his Heavenly Father's care and sovereign will? We had a long and storied history together, and I knew in my head my answer was: "Yes, Lord, I trust You and Your ways—even with my greatest vulnerability, my mentally handicapped son." I just needed my heart to fall in line. That would take time.

Yet time was my enemy. May 1, 2021, another date long-circled on our calendar, was upon us. But as the day dawned in the freshness of a spring morning, we were hardly prepared emotionally for the new chapter it elicited. Sure, we had everything packed and ready to go. We had borrowed a friend's truck and trailer. And with our own SUV as well, we managed to squeeze everything in for the journey across town. Mary and Ben availed themselves for the day to help settle Daniel

JOY CLINE

into his new digs. And with Logan, his parents, and sister, we were a full house indeed.

While we used the creepy staircase to cart some of Daniel's belongings up to his new place, we received permission for the day to use a much larger staircase that wound its way through the lower tenant's unit. It was a little awkward carting our larger furniture though their home in order to reach Logan and Daniel's upper unit, but it did enable us to meet the boys' new neighbors. We went around introducing ourselves and stating our associations.

"Hi, I'm Steve, and this is my wife Tina," the neighbor said, stretching out his hand for a shake. "We're Black." In the racially charged climate of the Twin Cities, less than a year removed from the death of George Floyd and all the riots, Steve's words caught me a little off guard. But he said it with a cackle that was both winsome and disarming. We instantly liked them and would come to learn they had hearts of gold. We couldn't have asked for better neighbors for the boys.

With the larger staircase at their disposal, the men were now able to haul up all of the larger furniture pieces. But one would prove obstinate. It was one of my best Facebook Marketplace finds...a brown Natuzzi Italian leather couch. The guys, working together, turned it this way and that. They measured and worked the math. They shoved, and grunted, and fumed as one hour turned into nearly two. For my part, I busied myself with the rest of the ladies in the kitchen while the couch drama unfolded. In my marriage to Geoff, I have found this the best strategy for tense moments such as these. At wit's end and with the towel about to be tossed, Logan imagined a nuance that at last succeeded.

SPECIAL

We arranged the rest of the house as best we could around the couch and the boys' specifications. When we felt the essentials were in place, we celebrated over Domino's pizza, and left the rest for Logan and Daniel's fine tuning.

When I next returned to the house, I marveled at what that fine tuning had yielded. They had transformed the place into a warm, inviting space, complete with a variety of houseplants that arched and climbed. Though decidedly masculine in its taste, Logan clearly had design skills. Logan also had another skill for which we were to find ourselves thankful. He was incredibly intentional. He made a point to find what was important to Daniel and met him there. The first full weekend they were in the house, he instituted movie and popcorn night…a Daniel standard. My boy was in heaven!

After moving Daniel and Logan in, it was not as if Geoff and I kicked up our heels at our newfound freedom. In fact, it was quite the opposite. Daniel's first few weeks required a bit of heavy lifting, so to speak, on our part. Logan was in his final push to graduation, so I stepped in to assist Daniel through this huge change.

JOY CLINE

In preparing for his launching, I had read a book, entitled *Gist: The Essence of Raising Life-Ready Kids,* co-authored by Michael W. Anderson and Timothy D. Johanson.[24] In it, the authors challenged me to identify just one to two things for Daniel to work on through this time of transition. Any more, they said, and it would become overwhelming and detrimental towards his growth. Heeding that advice, I decided what Daniel most needed to tackle was being able to independently get himself to and from Bethel each day.

That first week of May I loaded my bike in the car and drove to New Brighton to ride in with Daniel to work. I kept to my hideaway Bethel perch by day, only to emerge at the end of Daniel's work shift to ride with him back to his new house. I'd point out landmarks along the way, allowing him to take the lead as the week progressed. Building on his growth, I began the next week up at Bethel without my bike, serving merely as Daniel's security blanket…nearby, but not draping him with my presence. By the end of the week, I followed his course on Find My Friends from the comfort of home. He was flying solo!

A wise friend of a Down syndrome daughter once said to me, "You don't know what you don't know" about our kids with special needs. Sometimes you think they have something mastered, only to find they really don't; while other times you hover over them in helicopter mode, only to find your oversight misguided. They were perfectly able to be independent. That first day riding bikes with Daniel from his New Brighton home was one of those unexpected moments.

I had arranged to meet Daniel at the bike rack after work for the ride back to his place. In the morning we had locked our bikes together to the rack with his new bike lock we

---

[24] Anderson, M. W., & Timothy D. Johanson, M. D. (2019). *Gist: The essence of raising life-ready kids.* Tyndale House Publishers, Inc.

SPECIAL

had ordered from Amazon. It was a premium lock—titanium and very heavy. Ben had his locked bike stolen from an underground parking garage only a few years earlier, and we were determined Daniel's orange Specialized Crossroads bike wouldn't succumb to the same fate. When Daniel emerged that day, he handed me his keychain for me to unlock the bikes.

"Oh no, Buddy, that's *your* job," I said, handing the keys back to him.

But my, did he struggle to unlock that bike! He worked and worked on it for ten minutes or so until I sensed exasperation setting in. Unable to take it any longer, I snatched the keys back from him, saying, "Here, why don't you let me try." But I fared no better. This premium lock was also a premium hassle. Finally, managing to fit the key just right, the chain clanked loudly away. I knew then the new lock wasn't going to see a day two. I handed the keychain back to Daniel.

Thankful for that being behind us, we were happy to just be on our bikes and riding. When we got to the house, Daniel fished out the key for the padlocked storage shed, so he could store his bike. He looked at me, but I said, "No, you try."

He managed to unlock the shed without too much incident, although the door did become unhinged in the process. We righted it; but before Daniel even put his bike away, he managed to jam the long-handled padlock in such a way that it was permanently locked. Only removing it with a lock cutter would allow us access again.

Undeterred, I said, "It's okay, Daniel. We can keep your bike in the laundry room in the basement." I knew there was no way

JOY CLINE

either of us was hoisting it up the creepy stairway. "Where's your key to the basement?"

"It's in the house." Daniel took the steps two at a time, eager to finally be back in his domain after our setbacks. He went to unlock the door. It didn't budge. He tried again. Still nothing. He tried the other lock. Nothing.

Now I was becoming exasperated. "Here, let me try." But try as I might, I couldn't get the doors unlocked either. About to contact Logan, I gave it one last go and managed to finally make an entry. Daniel was visibly relieved, but also shaken by the difficulty of all these locks. In my head, I figured it was the combination of the door lock and deadbolt that had confounded us. I determined to talk to Logan about locking only the deadbolt in the future to simplify things for Daniel.

"Now where's that laundry key, Daniel?" He snatched it from the key holder and together we went to put his bike in the basement storage. But Daniel couldn't even *get* the key into the basement lock. He tried and tried. It didn't seem to even fit.

"You can't be serious!" I snapped impatiently. I snatched the key once again and turned it both ways, willing it to fit. "Are you *sure* this is the key to the basement?"

"I think so."

Considering my options for storing the bike, I jiggled the key some more. Somehow miraculously, it clicked in and turned. I heaved the bike down the steps and into an empty corner, depositing it with thud. Already I was inwardly psyching myself up for doing this all again in the morning. Daniel's confidence clearly shot and my own not far behind, I knew we had found

SPECIAL

our number two from the book on the things for Daniel to work on: locks. "You don't know what you don't know."

With persistence, new locks, and strategies, Daniel finally did master the locks in his life, as well as the commute to Bethel. And by the time summer was ending and he was heading back to Bethel for work, the county had conveniently awarded him a Lyft pass allowing him a credit on the Lyft app. With Logan's help, Daniel found it decidedly easier to click and summon a Lyft driver than to ride his bike and lock it at Bethel or in the shed. Smart kid. He never looked back, nor did he ever ride his bike to Bethel again.

Daniel found living with Logan to be stimulating. Besides being a decorating whiz and incredibly intentional, Logan was an all-around cool guy. He wore cool clothes and did cool things. He also seemed unflappable, which I chalked up to his psychology degree. With Daniel, he had a lot of opportunities to put it into practice. At one point he said to us, "Man! Can he talk a lot!" So much so, it seemed, Logan had to institute quiet study time, just so he could get his seminary school work done. Fortunately, Jan, Daniel's Math and Finances professor from his BUILD days, supplied Daniel with homework so he, too, could do his school work alongside Logan. Amazingly, she even corrected his homework and gave him feedback, even though he was no longer a student. That's just Bethel. That's just Jan.

Over time, Logan's studious ways would earn him a new moniker from neighbor Steve, who began referring to Logan as "the Professor." By now, Steve, Tina, and their family had become part of the fabric of living at 704 10th St. NW, particularly for Daniel. He talked to them when he got the mail, giving any junk mail to Steve to burn in his frequent bonfires. They let Daniel play with their dog Oreo when he needed a

JOY CLINE

puppy fix. Steve even kept the boys well stocked with pop for movie nights from his job at a Pepsi distribution center. More importantly for me as a mom, they became his staunch overseers. They took note any time he left the house alone, making sure they also saw him arrive safely back home. They made him feel safe and cared for, particularly when Logan was away at work or school. Daniel knew he could count on Steve and Tina.

One early summer night when Logan was off leading a youth Bible study, the weather grew nasty. From an early age, Daniel has had a heightened obsession with weather. He gets it from his sister Mary, who once aspired to be a meteorologist. As with sports, it's one of his go-to conversation starters, particularly when the mundane gives way to the extreme. This obsession, I'm sure, is from being awakened by sirens on summer nights and rushed to the basement. It's the result of watching too many WCCO storm updates while waiting for warnings to pass. No doubt, severe weather excites him. But inwardly, it also scares him. This particular night, the weather was decidedly dicey. So dicey, in fact, a tornado warning had been issued for Daniel's county. Seeing this, Geoff and I called Daniel to talk him through his fears and give him some directives. But even as we were on the phone with him, we heard a distant knocking. It was Steve at Daniel's door.

"Come on, Daniel. Join me and the family in the basement until this storm blows over." Daniel didn't need a second invitation. He hung up on us and scampered down the stairs behind Steve to safety.

Even as Steve and Tina invited Daniel into their lives, so much more so did Logan. He brought him along to hang out with his friends, the same friends he had originally planned to room with after graduation. As Bethel guys, Daniel knew them too

SPECIAL

and thrilled at the inclusion of it all. Logan brought Daniel to his Eden Prairie home for dinners with his family, where Steve and Tiffany Fisco welcomed him as one of their own. Logan also had Daniel tag along for volunteering opportunities at the church where he was interning. Together, they led games for Vacation Bible School, helped with a back-to-school supplies drive, and worked at a food kitchen. I thought how Daniel had come full circle with church, from being served to being the server. Those times of trying to find Daniel's place at church seemed such a distant memory now.

As Bethel grads, Logan also made sure the two of them took full advantage of the nearby university and its facilities. They worked out in the Wellness Center and attended Sunday night Vespers from time to time. Logan even proved a gourmet cook, enlarging Daniel's palette by introducing him to salmon and sushi. Daniel had been a decidedly hamburger, pizza, and pasta guy! Between changing his diet and regularly working out with him, it was as if Logan had become Daniel's personal trainer on *The Greatest Loser*. And it yielded some pretty impressive results! Daniel dropped a whopping fifteen pounds to tip the scales at his lowest weight in years! He looked trim and fit. But Logan treated Daniel like more than a personal

JOY CLINE

trainer, even more than a Rumi roommate. He treated him like a friend. Daniel was truly living his best life in the revelry of it all.

Yet time inevitably evokes change. Now into their second summer living together, Logan had decided not to continue at seminary and had instead accepted a new job. Through frugal management of his income, Logan had managed to pay off nearly all of his college debt. These changes signaled the end. Logan informed us he was planning on moving out to live with his cousins at the end of August. Sixteen months....it had been a good run for Daniel. I think both boys, by then, had had their fill of mowing grass and shoveling snow. Enthusiasm definitely had waned.

As August neared its end, we invited the boys out to dinner at the Tavern for one last hurrah. We talked memories. We talked future plans. We talked logistics of the move ahead. It was the stuff of a mutual connection. Heading out to the cars afterwards, the weight of the moment seemed to overcome Logan. He turned and looked Daniel squarely in the eye.

"This isn't the end, you know. We're friends." And I knew it wasn't. For his glistening eyes exposed his earnestness. True to his word, Logan has remained intentional in the years since moving out, regularly calling Daniel to go out for dinner, see the latest Marvel movie, or meet his girlfriend. After all, that's what friends do.

20

HAVING PEOPLE

With word of his impending move, Logan left us nearly the entire summer to plot the next course for Daniel. His August end date was conveniently the end of their lease, setting us up for a natural progression to something new.

But what was that something new? And did we want Daniel to leave 704 10th St. NW? The place possessed some charm, creepy staircase and all! Certainly, the location was ideal for Daniel to get to his job. He had become acquainted with the area and felt comfortable navigating it. In fact, he was becoming a regular at the local library. There's just something about familiarity that is grounding, especially for a young man with autism. And in Steve and Tina, Daniel still had the best neighbors. They were almost like his unpaid support!

Knowing Daniel's level of comfort with his current living situation, Geoff and I contemplated how he might be able to stay in his upper unit. We didn't feel comfortable sticking with Rumi and bringing in an unknown roommate to replace Logan, even if they were vetted. We did, however, explore Mark Winter's idea for piecing together services with a living situation. We had the house. We just needed the help. Fortunately, we had a contact in the area for such services. We turned to Scott Rugel. Geoff and I had served together with Scott on BUILD's Advisory Committee. He also worked at Mary T. Inc., a company in the area which provided, among other things, in-home disability services.

JOY CLINE

When we reached out, Scott didn't mince words. He told us it was a difficult time to get staffing, as Mary T. Inc. was having a hard time securing needed help. It didn't surprise us. It seemed no one wanted to work any longer coming out of Covid. Daniel's need for staffing during the weekday hours, however, increased his chances. Scott said weekdays were decidedly easier to fill than nights or weekends—that, and the fact that Daniel was largely independent, needing only oversight for cleaning and help with shopping and meal prep. Making no promises, he told us he'd see what he could do.

As we barreled ever closer to the last day of July, the date by which we would need to either extend our lease or let the upper unit go, doubts crept into my mind. Having Daniel stay in his current place meant he would essentially be living on his own...no one to come back home to, no one with whom to share movie nights and Packers' games, no one to be there in case of an unforeseen emergency. That last one hit like a missile to my soul, unleashing a whole new set of what if's in me: what if there was a fire, what if Daniel locked himself out, what if he became lonely and withdrawn, what if his sickness returned. Of course, Steve and Tina were just down the stairs, but how much could we realistically lean on them as neighbors before overstepping boundaries?

Into those swirling doubts, I had invited Dawn for a visit. This meeting, however, needed no shove from Geoff. By now, she had become something more—that rare thing, a good friend. So when I asked her over, this was merely two friends catching up over tea, no hidden agenda. And while our conversation did eventually turn towards the sharing of my doubts, it was merely the stuff of a transparent relationship. But Dawn offered more, and I would once again glean from her wisdom. She heard my mother fears and proposed we ask our landlord for a two-month extension to our current lease. These two

SPECIAL

months could serve as a sort of trial run to gauge Daniel's readiness to navigate living all on his own, while also buying time for God to open, perhaps, another door. At the end, we prayed for just that.

Days later, Geoff and I prayed as well, bowing our heads over the phone between us and asking our heavenly Father to go before us in our conversation with Landlord Dan. We prayed for Dan's favor with our request and—if it be His will—that Daniel might be able to stay in the upper unit. What we were asking of Landlord Dan was audacious. It was a big ask. We thought how seemingly easy it had been to find renters last go round. Why would he consent to our wishes? Why would he acquiesce to renting to a mentally disabled young man? Why wouldn't he say "no?"

With our "amen," Geoff dialed Dan's number. I call Geoff winsome. He is magical in relating to people. He has this "golly, aw shucks" way about him that others find…well, winsome. And that is exactly why *he* was making the call and not me. Geoff skillfully laid out Daniel's situation and presented our request to Dan. It was met by a pregnant pause. Geoff jumped into the silence, sweetening the request with an offer to pay an additional $100 for each of those two months. Dan bit on it. Daniel had his two-month extension, which would now give us until the end of October to lock into a year lease or move on. The Lord once again clearly intervened for us in making the "audacious" possible.

We now had the place. And in the meantime, Scott had come through and scheduled an intake meeting with staff from Mary T. Inc. We were inching ever closer towards the support Daniel would need to live there. In the meeting, the two women asked Daniel lots of questions, trying to determine his level of care and the hours of support he would need. We would figure out

JOY CLINE

when those hours would be scheduled later, though they took copious notes on his availability.

Driving that availability was his job with Sodexo. As August was beginning to wind down, Daniel was just heading back to work…year three. This year, however, looked a little different. Beside him now, he had a girlfriend, Kirsta Graf, who just happened to work down the line serving desserts in Bethel's Dining Center. Kirsta, all 4'9" of her, is a dynamo. She's spunky, or—like she likes to say—she's got "sparkle." She has star power as a spokesperson for Jack's Basket, an international nonprofit elevating those with Down syndrome and working towards changing the narrative given at birth. And with her star power, she has the diva personality to match. She finished a strong second in Bethel's Got Talent with her sign language interpretation of Katy Perry's "Firework." While Kirsta craves the stage, Daniel runs as far from it as he can get. While Kirsta delivers emotive answers to questions, Daniel struggles for the words to convey his feelings. And while Kirsta has decided opinions about just about everything, Daniel's just happy to be along for the ride. But as they say…opposites attract. She and Daniel graduated together in 2019, as part of BUILD's Cohort Three. Yet for the two years they had attended Bethel together, they had been content merely as friends.

Something shifted as the two of them headed back to work at Sodexo's opening meeting for the 2022 school year. Proximity certainly had something to do with it. Daniel worked with Kirsta and lived a mere mile or so from the Graf's. He also was sporting a fresh haircut that day and looking quite buff from Logan's personal training magic. Whatever the case, I saw the sparkle in Kirsta as she locked eyes with Daniel with a fresh gaze. She scooted her chair a little closer to him in the meeting and took his arm, leaning into him to help her down the stairs. When the meeting was over, she moved to seal the deal.

SPECIAL

"Can Daniel come to my house to watch a movie?" Kirsta asked. Though not entirely sure what all went on with that movie, it was settled. From that day on, they were a pair.

Over two years later, they're still watching movies together. Though now it has a designated night—Mondays—and usually there's a big bowl of popcorn somewhere in the mix. They sit together on the couch. Kirsta often lays her head on Daniel's shoulder. Sometimes they hold hands. Their relationship has thrived over their compatibility and mutual love of movies, music, Packers football, and Jesus. Much has fallen on the shoulders of Dan and Alicia, Kirsta's parents, to uphold this budding romance. They cart the two of them here and there, and extend invites to Daniel on a whim, which he never turns down. And the thing about the Grafs…they don't think twice about it.

Even better, in dating Kirsta, Daniel has been enveloped into the larger Graf family circle. Whether for the family Halloween party or a hangout with the cousins over pizza, they extend the open door to Daniel as well. Kirsta's Auntie

JOY CLINE

Melissa serves as the pair's personal trainer, scheduling weekly workouts for them. She and husband Rick have even been known to have Daniel over for movie nights when Kirsta is out of town. And sometimes it's not even family, but the friends of the Grafs, who host the two of them. The Grafs have an incredibly wide net. In the distance between us, I'm simply grateful for all the companionship and for another set of motherly eyes on him.

So what looked like a lonely season for Daniel in the absence of having Logan under roof, suddenly became a very full one because of the Grafs. We tried to fill it too, in our own measly way. We had a standing nightly FaceTime date with him where we were able to catch up and have eyes on him ourselves, or at least eyes on his ceiling. Daniel hasn't gotten the knack for positioning his phone camera consistently. On one of these early FaceTime meetings, just into the trial lease period, Daniel was bubbling over with some news.

"Kelly and Aleks are moving across the street."

"Who are Kelly and Aleks?" I inquired, curious.

"You know, Kelly who works in Admissions, and Aleks, Kirsta's friend," Daniel said impatiently. He always assumes I know *exactly* who he's talking about. In this case, I actually did. Aleks was one of those "wide net" friends of the Grafs who was notorious for taking Kirsta to their high school prom. It had been traumatic for Kirsta when Aleks married Kelly. She instantly became the "other woman." Both Aleks and Kelly were also friends of Daniel's from his Bethel days. Knowing they were moving in across the street, the view from his second floor living room window suddenly became increasingly interesting. The blinds were left up, allowing the warm early September sun to come streaming in. He didn't want to miss any movement that might signal their arrival.

SPECIAL

Meanwhile, it was Labor Day weekend, and the Grafs went to the late Sunday morning service at Eaglebrook Church, a vast congregation that is the largest in Minnesota. It wasn't the service they typically attended. They sat down on the right side of the church, awaiting the start of the service. It wasn't long before Alicia's scanning eyes spotted friends Dan and Christine Westlund, Aleks' parents, just a few rows away. This was unusual. While good friends, they had never run into one another at church before. She waved and made a point to connect with them in the lobby afterwards.

"Guess what? Aleks and Kelly found a house!" Exclaimed Christine, saddling up alongside Dan and Alicia outside the auditorium doors.

"Where?" Asked Alicia.

"657 10th St. NW, in New Brighton."

"No way! That must be, like, right across the street from Daniel's house!"

"Daniel who?"

"Daniel Cline, Kirsta's boyfriend."

Alicia went on to fill in the backstory of Daniel for Christine and Dan. She added that he was currently living in his rental house alone for the next couple of months as he figured out his next move. A light clicked. Aleks and Kelly weren't merely moving across the street, they also had a rental unit on their property—a cute little one bedroom house. It currently had a tenant from the previous owner, but what if...? The wheels were turning!

JOY CLINE

I'm so glad we sat on the right side today!" Said Christine. "Usually we sit on the left! Totally, totally orchestrated by the Lord!"

"Totally!" Agreed Alicia, and the two went their separate ways. But the conversation lingered and eventually converged. Christine called Aleks and Kelly, who called Alicia, who called me, who called Kelly. And when the dust had cleared, Aleks and Kelly were wondering if Daniel just might like to move into their rental house, a mere thirty steps or so from their own home. A house! God had once again heard the desires of his heart, and opened a door for Daniel. His enthusiastic "yes" couldn't leap from his mouth fast enough!

What some might attribute to chance and coincidence, we knew otherwise. The two-month trial had protected Daniel from signing a year's lease, enabling him to be open for this better opportunity, an opportunity that came knocking just days into his trial period. On October 30th, he would be changing addresses again, but this time just across the street and a few digits off...to 655 10th St. NW.

Geoff and I asked Aleks and Kelly if they wanted to be something more than just Daniel's landlords. How would they like to also be his support? They thought that sounded great! So we called Mary T. Inc., informing them we had decided to go a different direction for Daniel's care. We called Landlord Dan, thanking him for his willingness to give us that two-month extension but telling him Daniel wouldn't be signing back on for another year. He had found another place. Both were hard calls for the gratitude we felt at the bridge they had provided, that bridge to something better that awaited just across the street.

SPECIAL

Though transitioning to a new location and new support is not for the faint of heart, we plowed through our mound of paperwork that transferred Daniel from his DD waiver to a Consumer-Directed Community Supports (CDCS) waiver to provide for his care and support. I'm sure there were moments in the process when Aleks and Kelly threw up their hands in exasperation, so daunting the paperwork and requirements. But they persevered—wholesome, good Midwestern stock they are, and—even more importantly—servants of Christ that they are. And as with Logan, Daniel's support wasn't merely someone punching a time card, they were friends that intimately cared for his well being. That has made all the difference.

When Steve and Tina found out Daniel was moving, they were disheartened. "What did we do?" They asked, as if sensing they hadn't somehow done their part to enable him to stay living above them. We reassured them it was quite the opposite! They had been the very reason we felt comfortable having him stay there for the two months after Logan's departure. For Daniel's part, he still went to visit them, and they still gave him a birthday present. But alas, by spring time they, too, had moved on to a new home.

Move-in day was decidedly easier than it had been when Daniel had moved in with Logan. Obviously, the move was shorter...just across the street. But even more so, it was due to the house being a single-story, tight space. He had a kitchen and dining area, a living room, bathroom, and bedroom—all the necessary parts, but the footprint was considerably smaller. So small, in fact, the prized brown Natuzzi Italian leather couch would have to be resold. The house simply had no room for a couch or for many of the other things Daniel had accumulated for his first move. Yet what it lacked in space, it

JOY CLINE

made up for in charm with its latching burnt orange windows and cozy nooks.

And while the loss of space remains a sacrifice, the people quotient far surpasses any sense of loss. Because for Daniel, after all these years, it's still about people. His example challenges me when I become a little too competitive or too caught up in my To Do list. It's all about people. Aleks and Kelly are his new people, and they live only a few steps away from a house he gets to call his own. And that makes me sleep well at night. God is good.

21

FLIGHT

In my life I have had several encounters with God—moments where I knew His unmistakable presence in a very tangible way. Often, it has been in the unexplainable, as circumstances deviated widely from the expected. Often, it has been in the voice of God that though inaudible, spoke with such clarity and authority I knew it to be Him. Always, these encounters have left me changed from my brush with the great I AM.

One of these encounters occurred at one of our most challenging seasons with Daniel, offering me a beacon of hope when the future seemed all but dim. It was the summer after his first year in middle school…after the IEP meeting that sent me reeling, and just months before the mysterious illness's furious debut and Daniel's humiliating shove at a classmate's hand. It came unexpectedly in the commonplace of summer garden work. And perhaps even more surprisingly for my nature, in my willingness to be drawn away from my work.

It was hard not to, so insistent the chatter that lured me in. Its persistence begged for an audience, and I deemed to determine the source of such clamor. I spied some sparrows perched in the branches of a young maple tree, their chirping reaching decibels of alarm. My eyes scanned to find the intended focus of all their racket—a young bird in the grass beyond attempting flight. As my presence threatened him, he made several unsuccessful leaps, flapping madly and eliciting an intensifying crescendo from his family. One more try and

JOY CLINE

he was airborne. His flight was hardly one of wonder. It was choppy with uncharacteristic dips. But somehow he navigated his way to the family tree and hung on for dear life.

The birds quieted, and I turned away, certain my magical brush with nature was over. But before long, the chorus of chirping resumed. I left the garden a second time to survey the lawn, spying yet another baby bird teetering in the thick grass some twenty feet beyond, his insistent chirps betraying his location. This baby bird appeared even more immature than his sibling—his undeveloped plumage, the tale tell sign. He responded to his cheering section with some hops and flaps of his own. But despite a mighty effort, the air eluded him. I thought, perhaps, I might encourage flight by moving towards him, as I had with his sibling. But alas, my proximity only served to heighten the cacophony from the branches beyond and chase the baby bird out into the street, grounded still, but now in a very vulnerable spot.

I retreated once again to my garden, saddened by the baby bird's likely demise and by my own inability to somehow rescue him from it. But try as I might, I couldn't focus on the work at hand. The still unfolding drama tugged at me. I needed closure.

The sight I returned to would stick with me forever. It was unbelievable. It was an anomaly. It was a miracle. Encouraged by his squad of cheerleaders, the baby bird had made his way from the street back into the grass. But this time would be different. For instead of futile attempts at flight, he had found an alternative route to the heights. With his vice-like feet and beak, and his wings for balance, he began the ascent up the young tree trunk to his awaiting family. He pecked and pulled, pecked and pulled, pecked and pulled, gripping the trunk with all the strength he could muster. His earnest effort astounded

SPECIAL

me. I found myself joining his family in cheering him along, willing him up that tree. With one final heave, he reached the lowest branch, hoisting himself up to its safety.

Now I don't know about you, but before that day I had never seen a baby bird climb up a tree, nor have I ever seen one since. It was unconventional, a deviance from what you'd normally expect. And when it was over, I felt privileged to bear witness to it. Yet I also knew God *meant* for me to be there to witness it. For I saw in the solemnity of the moment from this family of birds comparisons to my own children, who at the time were entering the public schools for the first time. Flight was just as elusive for them at times, as they sought to establish themselves from their inauspicious homeschooling roots.

Yet as time went by, the birds' flights would also take on a far broader inference to my children's flight from our home nest. Mary and Ben have now long since left the nest on their solo flights toward independence. Neither were without dips and choppy moments along the way, unleashing from me some of my patented gasps they're so fond of. But while not perfect, their flight paths have been fairly, well, ordinary...college, jobs, new homes, families. Their soaring ways, though expected, still make me proud.

Daniel's flight path has been distinctly different. Much like the obstacles the last baby bird faced because of his immaturity, Daniel has fought the grounding his disabilities have wrought. He has been ridiculed for his differentness, ostracized because of his inability to compete on a normal playing field, preyed upon by those who needed to substantiate their own worth at his expense, and limited by those who failed to see his potential. That last one, in particular, played out over and over. But Daniel didn't succumb to its grounding ways. And in so doing, he stared down the naysayers who diminished what he could become.

He may have put a strain on a Sunday School class by his mere attendance, but he learned to lead children in VBS games… peck and pull. He may have struggled to keep pace in classes with his homeschool peers, but he found acceptance in the classrooms of Bethel University…peck and pull. He may have been stymied by his vulnerabilities, but availed himself to stretching experiences that grew his confidence…peck and pull. He may have been bullied and mocked for being different, but he was awarded a crown for his resilience…peck and pull. And he may have been told at nine years old to start looking for a group home, but has found living on his own quite to his liking…peck and pull—a miraculous ascent indeed!

Certainly Daniel hasn't made this ascent alone. He has had his own set of cheerleaders alongside for the flight—family, friends, teachers, coaches, and aides who know Daniel intimately and recognize these accomplishments, however small in the world's eyes, are indeed flight and not merely an arduous climb. This is a testament to God whose deliberate hand enabled an unorthodox flight towards independence. And this is a testament to the Unsinkable Daniel Cline, whose resilience and inextinguishable smile propelled him to unexpected heights. Keep soaring, my dear son, keep soaring!

"Now to him who is able to do immeasurably more than all we ask or imagine, according to his power that is at work within us, to him be glory in the church and in Christ Jesus throughout all generations, for ever and ever!"[25]

---

[25] *Bible gateway passage: Ephesians 3:20-21 - new international version.* Bible Gateway. (n.d.-e). https://www.biblegateway.com/passage/?search=Ephesians+3%3A20-21&version=NIV

EPILOGUE

Originally, my hope in writing this book was to preserve our family stories of God's faithfulness for my children and for generations of Clines yet to come—to somehow encapsulate a history as a marker for their own faith in times of testing against insurmountable odds. Somewhere along the way, however, it also became my hope and mission to elevate Daniel—and the so many others like him—who continue to be marginalized and passed by in our society.

Yet walking through these stories again in their penning, God had something for me as well. It came in the form of a song that became, of sorts, an anthem for my own voiced confession:

When did I start to forget
All of the great things You did?
When did I throw away faith for the impossible?
How did I start to believe
You weren't sufficient for me?
Why do I talk myself out of seeing miracles?

The lyrics of Elevation Worship's *More Than Able* haunted me on a profound level. They gave voice to my own unsettled conviction that despite this long history I was amassing of God getting our family through challenges over and over and over, I still questioned His ability in my todays. Without fail, every time I heard the song play, the nail went deeper, and I wept. I wept over the admission of my own faithlessness despite the mounting evidence of His great faithfulness. Greater still, I wept that even as I sought the increase of generational faith by the retelling of these stories, my own faith yet lagged.

You are more than able
You are more than able
You are more than able
You are more than able
Who am I to deny what the Lord can do?[26]

While in my head I knew the truth of these words, the greater surgery was relegated to my heart. It was a faith issue, and God was growing mine. Like the father in Mark 9 who sought out Jesus' healing for his son who was tormented by evil spirits, I had to acknowledge my lacking.

"What do you mean, 'If I can'?" Jesus asked. "Anything is possible if a person believes."

The father instantly cried out, "I do believe, but help me overcome my unbelief!"[27]

The father's admission became mine as well.

This book is the reminder for me to declare in confidence with the words of the song: "You are more than able. Who am I to deny what the Lord can do?"

"Now faith is confidence in what we hope for and assurance about what we do not see."[28]

That is faith indeed...perfect it in me, Lord.

---

[26] Google. (n.d.-a). Google search. https://www.google.com/search?q=more%2Bthan%2Bable%2Blyrics&ie=UTF-8&oe=UTF-8&hl=en-us&client=safari

[27] *Bible gateway passage: Mark 9:23-24 - new international version.* Bible Gateway. (n.d.-g). https://www.biblegateway.com/passage/?search=Mark+9%3A23-24&version=NIV

[28] *Bible gateway passage: Hebrews 11:1 - new international version.* Bible Gateway. (n.d.-f). https://www.biblegateway.com/passage/?search=Hebrews+11%3A1&version=NIV

DISCLAIMER

The stories in this book reflect the author's recollection of events. Some names, locations, and identifying characteristics have been changed to protect the privacy of those depicted. Dialogue has been re-created from memory in some cases as well.

Made in the USA
Monee, IL
27 May 2025